# Frida Kahlo *and* Diego Rivera

## Their Lives *and* Ideas

•••

# 24 activities

•••

CAROL SABBETH

CHICAGO REVIEW PRESS

*To my brother, John Landstrom*

**Library of Congress Cataloging-in-Publication Data**
Sabbeth, Carol, 1957–
    Frida Kahlo and Diego Rivera—their lives and ideas :
24 activities / Carol Sabbeth.—1st ed.
        p. cm.
        Includes bibliographical references and index.
        ISBN 1-55652-569-9
        1. Art—Study and teaching (Elementary)—Activity programs.
2. Kahlo, Frida—Appreciation. 3. Rivera, Diego, 1886–1957—
Appreciation. I. Title.

ND350.S25 2005
759.972—dc22

                                                        2004024525

Cover and interior design: Joan Sommers Design
Interior illustrations: TJ Romero

© 2005 Carol Sabbeth
All rights reserved
First edition
Published by Chicago Review Press, Incorporated
814 North Franklin Street
Chicago, Illinois 60610
ISBN 1-55652-569-9
Printed in China
5  4  3  2  1

**About the Author**
Carol Sabbeth presents art workshops to children and teachers throughout the United States. She also performs as a storyteller, bringing art history to life by impersonating famous women artists. She teaches at the American School of Paris's summer program, and is author of *Monet and the Impressionists for Kids*, *Crayons and Computers*, and *Kids' Computer Creations*. She lives in Roswell, Georgia, with her husband, Alex.

# Acknowledgments

A heartfelt thanks to those who have shared their knowledge, enthusiasm, and support. Sylvia Inwood, Linda and Michael Margolin, Lucilla Ruvalcaba, Alyson Plotsky, Angela Villalba, Elena Climent, and Laura Brannen contributed their time and expertise. As always, I appreciate the creative and professional talent of Cynthia Sherry and Lisa Rosenthal, along with Gerilee Hundt, Allison Felus, and Brooke Kush. And to Joan Sommers and Sommers Design. A big thank you to Ira Gonzalez. Born in Mexico City, she was a great advisor and ambassador for her country. And to her mother, Maricarmen Vargas de Gonzalez. Last, to my husband, Alex, who shared his talent and enthusiasm every step of the way. *Muchas gracias mis amigos.*

# Contents

# Time Line

**1886** Diego Rivera is born in Guanajuato, Mexico, on December 8

**1896** Rivera begins art classes at Mexico City's San Carlos Academy of Fine Arts

**1907** Rivera travels to Spain to study art; later, he moves to Paris

Frida Kahlo is born in Coyoacán, Mexico, on July 6

**1910** The Mexican Revolution begins (ends in 1920)

**1911** Porfirio Díaz resigns as president of Mexico and escapes to France

**1913** Doctors diagnose Kahlo with polio

**1914** World War I begins in Europe (ends in 1918)

**1920** Álvaro Obregón is elected president of Mexico

**1921** Rivera returns to Mexico and begins his mural-painting career

**1922** Kahlo attends the National Preparatory School

**1925** On September 17, Kahlo is seriously injured in a trolley accident

**1929** Kahlo and Rivera marry

The stock market crashes in the United States, beginning the era known as the Great Depression

**1930** Kahlo and Rivera make their first visit to the United States

**1931** Rivera paints murals in San Francisco, California; Kahlo paints *Portrait of Luther Burbank*; and New York's Museum of Modern Art's exhibition of Rivera's work

**1932** Kahlo and Rivera travel to Detroit where he paints murals at the Detroit Institute of Arts

**1933** Rivera begins a mural in New York City for Rockefeller; Kahlo paints *My Dress Hangs There*

**1934** Kahlo and Rivera return to Mexico

**1937** Leon Trotsky arrives in Mexico with his wife, Natalia; they move into the Casa Azul

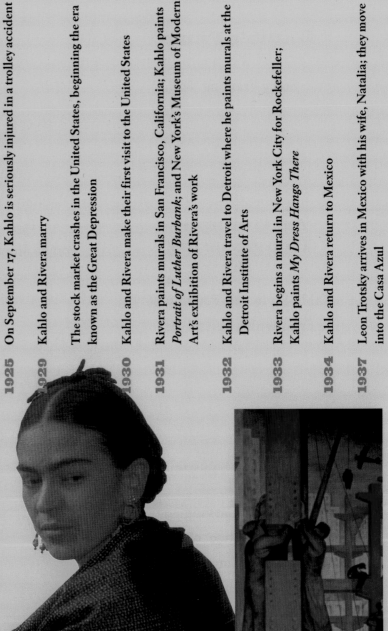

**1938** Kahlo travels to New York for her first solo art exhibition

**1939** Kahlo travels to Paris where she participates in an exhibition titled *Mexique*; the Louvre buys her self-portrait, *The Frame*—she is the first Mexican artist added to their permanent collection

Kahlo returns home to learn that Rivera wants a divorce; they divorce in November

World War II begins

**1940** Rivera returns to San Francisco to participate in the *Art in Action* exhibition at the Golden Gate International Exposition

Trotsky is assassinated

Kahlo and Rivera are remarried in San Francisco

**1941** Kahlo returns to live at the family home, the Casa Azul; Rivera joins her when he returns from San Francisco

**1942** Rivera begins to build Anahuacalli

**1943** Kahlo and Rivera begin teaching at La Esmeralda

**1950** Kahlo spends most of the year in the hospital because of spinal surgery and infections

**1953** In April, Kahlo has a solo exhibition in Mexico City

In July, her right leg is amputated below the knee because of gangrene

**1954** Kahlo dies on July 13

**1957** Rivera dies on November 24

**1958** The Casa Azul opens to the public as the Frida Kahlo Museum

**1965** Anahuacalli opens to the public

vii

*Frieda and Diego Rivera,*
Frida Kahlo, 1931

# Life at the Casa Azul

On a quiet street in Mexico City there's a bright blue house called the Casa Azul. Even though nobody lives there, visitors flock to the house. Today, it's a museum. Sixty or so years ago, it was home to Mexico's two most celebrated artists, Frida Kahlo and Diego Rivera.

Imagine strolling by the house on Londres Street on a warm Mexican evening in the summer of 1941. You will find a magical environment hidden behind these vivid blue walls. Stepping through the doorway, you enter the garden. A parrot might land on top of your head and welcome you with an enthusiastic call in Spanish. A baby deer might leap across your path as a cat nuzzles your ankles. Meanwhile, an energetic monkey will likely climb into your arms to give you a hug.

As you pass through the lush garden filled with caged song-birds and ancient stone carvings, you hear raucous laughter coming from inside the house. Peeking into an open window, you might spy a lively group gathered around the table. A huge mountain of a man is holding court. That's Diego Rivera. He's probably entertaining his guests with a dramatic tall tale—most likely about himself. Or maybe the conversation is about politics. Whatever the topic, his petite wife, Frida Kahlo, will loudly interject her own comments, or she may even break into one of her beloved *corridos* (Mexican folk songs).

Perhaps you'll recognize some of the guests. Mexico's most beautiful movie star, Dolores del Rio, is sitting next to American gangster film star Edward G. Robinson. Other guests are French surrealist André Breton and one of the richest men in America, John D. Rockefeller. Art lovers and artists the world over made it a point to visit Kahlo and Rivera whenever they traveled to Mexico.

If Fulang-Chang, one of Kahlo's pet monkeys, spots a juicy piece of fruit, watch out! He'll leap out of your arms and right onto the table. Grabbing the fruit, he'll quickly make off with his bounty. Such a sight will only surprise first-time visitors; others will be thankful that Bonito (Kahlo's pet parrot) isn't waddling his way through the treats, nibbling at everyone's plate. Meanwhile, the hosts will delight in the antics of their guests and their pets.

Like the artists who lived there, the Casa Azul was anything but dull.

## Viva Mexico!

Frida Kahlo was actually born at the Casa Azul. Diego Rivera was born in Guanajuato, a beautiful town in the mountains of Mexico. They lived during a time when Mexico was undergoing many changes, including a revolution. Both Rivera and Kahlo were politically active. They were determined to do whatever they could to improve their country. Most of all, they wanted poor people to have better lives.

To show his concern, Rivera made bold statements through his art. He painted huge murals in Mexico and the United States. He used his paintbrush to give life to his ideas about social issues. Sometimes, his painting got him into trouble. Controversy followed him everywhere . . . and he loved it!

In addition to murals, Rivera also painted many canvases, often showing the dignity of Mexico's poor. Some of his most famous paintings are of Mexican peasants carrying baskets filled with flowers.

Although Kahlo was politically outspoken, her art was more personal. Her small paintings, many of them self-portraits, are packed with emotion. She loved life and had a wild, playful personality. In her colorful native Mexican costumes and dazzling silver and jade jewelry, she looked like a work of art herself.

Kahlo and Rivera were two of the world's most celebrated artists. Why was Rivera's art so controversial? What caused Kahlo to paint her dreamlike, and sometimes sad, pictures? *Frida Kahlo and Diego Rivera* tells you about the artists' lives, their art, and their ideas. It also creates a portrait of the ways in which Mexico influenced their art.

You'll learn what it was like to live in Mexico 100 years ago. During this time, artists such as José Guadalupe Posada created wonderful works. He's famous for his playful cartoons that feature skeletons. You'll see how he (and his creation Catrina) influenced the art of Kahlo and Rivera.

Other Mexican artists inspired Kahlo and Rivera as well. You'll learn how Rivera collected the art of the Aztecs, Mayans, and other ancient Mexican cultures. He gave lectures proclaiming the talents of the ancient artisans, and he built a museum to honor them. You'll find out about Kahlo's favorite type of art, Mexican folk art. You'll also visit the outdoor market and celebrate Kahlo's favorite Mexican holidays, such as Day of the Dead.

The artists traveled to other countries too. See the murals and hear the stories behind Rivera's San Francisco, Detroit, and New York frescoes. And watch Kahlo's rise to fame in the United States and Europe.

Throughout the book are 24 activities inspired by Kahlo, Rivera, and the nation of Mexico. Try them out as you learn about two fabulous artists who caused quite a stir during their lifetimes and who continue to inspire and fascinate us today.

Kahlo and Rivera, 1938, Coyoacán

*The Making of a Fresco
Showing the Building of a City,*
Diego Rivera, April–June 1931

# 1 Diego Rivera—The Fiesta Begins!

Wherever Diego Rivera went, he created a stir. His first visit to San Francisco in 1930 was no exception. His fame as a muralist had spread throughout Mexico. Now a group of art patrons from the United States commissioned him to decorate their walls, too.

Squeezed into the back of a tiny sports car, he waved his arms with excitement at what he saw. Anyone watching the green convertible zip up and down the impossibly steep streets had to smile. Rivera wore a Stetson hat that made his 300-pound, six-foot frame seem even larger. It was like sightseeing on a roller coaster—it seemed as if he might fly out of the car at any moment.

The sights he saw were thrilling! Construction workers, perched high atop steel beams, were building skyscrapers. Small airplanes crisscrossed above the bay. On the ground, men in overalls operated machines, while engineers studied blueprints. They were building San Francisco, and Diego Rivera, the great Mexican muralist, was there to paint them.

At the bottom of Chestnut Street, one of the steepest streets in the city, was his mural. It was a large interior wall of an art school. Rivera covered the wall with a type of mural called a fresco. A fresco is made by applying paint to damp plaster. As the plaster dries, the colors bond to it.

Rivera titled his creation *The Making of a Fresco Showing the Building of a City*. He included himself in the painting, and his assistants busy with their tasks. One man spreads fresh plaster while others measure the wall. In the center sits the master himself, Rivera. His back is to us, and his plump bottom hangs over the scaffold. He's doing what he loves best—painting a mural.

## An Artist Is Born

On December 8, 1886, twin boys were born in the Mexican village of Guanajuato (gwan-e-HWAT-tow), located in the Sierra Madre Mountains.

The arrival of two babies caused tremendous excitement in the household of Señor Diego and Señora María Rivera. In the four years of their marriage, María had been pregnant four times. The first three births ended tragically when she delivered stillborn (lifeless) babies. Now, the neighbors heard the cries of a newborn coming from the Rivera home. The doctor came out of the bedroom and held up two fingers.

Two? There were two babies? Señor Rivera was overjoyed!

But the doctor had more news. It was not good. This time there had been a different tragedy during delivery. In 1886 it

## Long Names Are a Tradition in Mexico

In Mexico, there is a tradition of giving babies very long names. Frida Kahlo's full name was Magdalena Carmen Frida Kahlo y Calderón. Her parents chose her first three names. In Mexico, parents often select names of a relative, such as a grandparent, or the name of a saint to use as first names.

Mexicans have two last names. The first is the father's family name. The second is the mother's family name. In Frida's case, Kahlo was her father's family name. Calderón was her mother's family name. Often *y* is inserted between these names; it means "and" in Spanish.

Traditionally, when a woman marries, she changes her name. She drops her mother's family name and adds the family name of her husband. Between these names is the word *de*, which means "of." Therefore, Frida Kahlo y Calderón became Frida Kahlo de Rivera when she married.

Confused? Try it out! If you don't already have a name that fits the formula, here's how you would change it: Your first name(s) + your father's last name + *y* + your mother's maiden name.

Diego Rivera, detail from *The Making of a Fresco Showing the Building of a City*, April–June 1931

was common for women to give birth at home. But giving birth was a risk for the mother. Having twins was an even greater risk.

Diego was the first. His mother bled badly during his birth. By the time his brother arrived a few minutes later, María had lost so much blood that she went into a coma. When the doctor failed to find her pulse, he pronounced her dead.

But a short while after the doctor left, María's friend leaned over to kiss her cold forehead and say good-bye. When she thought she heard María breathing, she cried out. They called the doctor back for a second opinion.

This time they gave María the blister test, the standard procedure for such a dilemma in those days. The doctor lit a match and placed it just beneath her left heel. To his great surprise, a blister formed. This wouldn't have happened if his original diagnosis had been correct. The babies' mother was alive! Eventually she made a full recovery.

### The City of Silver

Rivera's parents were well-educated schoolteachers who met in Guanajuato. His mother was a small woman of Spanish and native Mexican heritage. His father was a large black-bearded man whose ancestors came from Europe. Rivera's grandfather

moved to Mexico from Spain. Diego's grandmother was of Portuguese-Jewish ancestry. As an adult, Diego liked to brag that he was a mixture of many cultures.

Today, Guanajuato is a charming old silver-mining town. It is located in central Mexico, 221 miles northwest of Mexico City. It was once Mexico's greatest silver-mining city.

The Riveras lived on the top floor of a beautiful house. It had a splendid view overlooking the rooftops of the town and the mountains beyond. The house was full of books. It had a grand piano in the drawing room. The Rivera family was wealthy enough to have a horse and carriage and a groom to drive them around town.

And now there were two more in the family. The firstborn was named Diego after his father. His bother was named Carlos. When it came time for Diego to be baptized, his parents gave him a very long name: Diego María de la Concepción Juan Nepomuceno Estanisloa de la Rivera y Barrientos Acosta y Rodríguez.

Each baby had his own nanny. Even with this special care, Carlos became very ill and died before his second birthday. After the funeral, Diego's mother wouldn't leave the child's grave. It didn't seem to matter that she still had Diego. In fact, she seemed to forget about him. She wouldn't leave Carlos, even at night. So Señor Rivera had to rent a room for his wife in the cemetery keeper's lodge.

María's doctor warned Señor Rivera that she might not recover. The only hope, the doctor suggested, was to distract her with work. He suggested that María go back to school.

Gradually, her husband persuaded her to continue her studies. She chose obstetrics, a branch of medicine that deals with pregnancy and childbirth. María wanted to be a midwife, someone who assists in childbirth. That way, she'd be able to help women who had similar problems to those she had experienced while giving birth.

María's studies left her no time for her young child. Luckily the family had Antonia, baby Diego's nurse, to watch over him.

## Ruled by a Dictator

Ten years before Diego was born, a general named Porfirio Díaz became president of Mexico. Although he called himself a president, he was a ruthless dictator. If anyone questioned his decisions, he silenced them by force. Because he was able to rig the voting, he was reelected many times and ruled Mexico for 35 years. This part of Mexico's history is called the *Porfiriato*.

With the help of foreign investment, Díaz modernized the country. He built railroads and roads. He set up telephone lines. The mining and oil industries prospered, too. Despite these contributions, there were many problems.

Díaz's rule came at a cost for most of Mexico's citizens. He made laws that kept rich people rich and poor people poor. Only a few wealthy Mexicans and foreign businesspeople profited from Díaz's reign.

The gap between the rich and the poor grew at an alarming rate. For example, many farmers lost their land to a handful of wealthy families who amassed huge plantations called *haciendas*. Thousands of peasants whose families had farmed the same acres for generations could not show legal title to their land. To enlarge their farms, the hacienda owners simply moved boundary markers, and occupied the peasant farmer's land. These powerful families used their influence with the local government to get approval for this illegal practice.

The hacienda owners often hired the very people whose land they had taken, and paid them terrible wages. As a result, the workers couldn't always afford food and housing. They often had to borrow money from the hacienda owners just to survive. The owners didn't allow the workers to leave the hacienda until all debts were paid. In this way, the workers became slaves to the landowners.

In the mining town where the Riveras lived, there were similar problems. Díaz permitted the mine owners to pay their employees extremely low wages, and the working conditions were horrible. The owners of the mines didn't care, and neither did Díaz. When the workers organized any kind of a protest, Díaz sent soldiers to suppress them. He didn't appreciate journalists like Rivera's father publicizing these problems.

When Rivera was 16, he was expelled from school for participating in an anti-Díaz demonstration. It would not be until late 1910, when Rivera was 24, that Díaz finally lost power. In the north, Francisco "Pancho" Villa led a rebellion in an attempt to overthrow the government. In the south, a peasant named Emiliano Zapata led landless farmers on hit-and-run attacks against wealthy plantations. It was the start of the Mexican Revolution. The ragtag army of revolutionaries lead by Villa, Zapata, and others eventually forced Díaz to surrender power.

## The Tale of a Goat

At age two, Diego was also not so healthy. He was too thin. He had rickets, a disease that affects the bones of children if they don't get proper nutrition. Diego needed to be fattened up!

The doctor advised that Diego be sent to the country. There, he could live a healthy outdoor life. Antonia was the answer. With the Riveras' blessing, she took Diego up into the mountains to her own village. With Diego strapped to her back, Antonia rode a donkey into the hills. He lived with Antonia and her family for two years.

When Diego was an adult, he wrote about this time with Antonia, who was a full-blooded Mexican Indian. Diego later wrote that he loved her more than his own mother. Her house was a primitive shack in the middle of the woods. He thought of her as something of a witch doctor because she practiced medicine with herbs and magic.

Antonia knew just how to fatten little Diego up. She found him another nanny—a nanny goat. His goat became an affectionate companion, and Diego had a lot of fresh goat's milk. Whether it was the magic, the goat's milk, or just plain love and attention, it worked. Diego began to thrive and became a chubby toddler.

Later in his life, Diego told stories about playing in the forest around Antonia's home. He and his goat were inseparable. When he roamed in the woods, Diego said, his goat always followed. She was like a mother watching over him. He imagined all the animals in the forest were his friends, even the dangerous and poisonous ones. Snakes and jaguars were his buddies, he claimed. Diego had a vivid imagination, and was famous for his tall tales. His memories of the forest were happy ones. Throughout his life Rivera loved animals. He once wrote, "I have always enjoyed the trust of animals—a precious gift."

After two years of Antonia's care, she returned a fat, healthy boy to the Rivera family. María wasn't thrilled that her son had changed into "another Diego." She didn't like that he spoke to his parrot in Antonia's native language, Tarascan (Ta-RAS-kan), instead of Spanish. But she was happy to have her family together. A year later, María gave birth to a baby girl. The Riveras named her María, after her mother.

## The Little Artist

By the time he was four years old, Diego was a very busy artist. He grabbed whatever pens and pencils he could find around the house, and drew on everything! When he couldn't find paper, he'd use the furniture and walls. His father appreciated Diego's enthusiasm, but he worried that his son might destroy the house. Finally, he covered the walls of

one room with canvas, and gave Diego a box of crayons and pencils. Diego had his first art studio.

In addition to drawing, Diego liked to play with model trains and other mechanical toys. It's likely that these toys didn't last very long since the first thing he did with a new toy was take it apart to see how it worked. After examining the interior mechanics of a toy, Diego would stand in front of his canvas-covered wall and draw a picture of his new treasure. He later called these pictures his first murals.

He loved real trains, too. Because of this fascination, he was nicknamed the Engineer. One of Diego's first drawings, done when he was only two or three, was of a locomotive and caboose chugging uphill.

## A Father's Influence

Diego's father was a schoolteacher and a city council member. At the time Diego was born, his father had a job inspecting rural schools. He liked the job, and believed schools were very important for the poor villages. He thought that with an education, children in these villages might be able to overcome their poverty. Señor Rivera wanted to help them.

But his journeys by horseback to the remote countryside upset him. There he found people

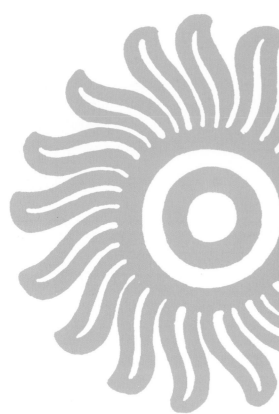

even more poverty-stricken than he had imagined. He decided to do something about it. He began writing for a newspaper called *El Demócrata*. He wrote about the horrible living conditions he witnessed. His articles regularly asked the wealthy people of Guanajuato to help. And he criticized the government for not doing more. (When young Diego grew up, he too would be very concerned about the poor.)

Unfortunately, Señor Rivera's pleas for the needy were mostly ignored. Part of the problem was his timing—the village's riches depended on its silver mines. Lately, the miners struggled to bring out enough silver from the mines to make a profit. Even the wealthy were now threatened. The whole town, from the shopkeepers to the mine owners, was affected. Guanajuato had become economically depressed.

During these hard times, charity became an unpopular subject. Señor Rivera's newspaper columns began to make his readers angry. But that didn't stop him. When he realized that his articles were being criticized, Rivera's father became even more rebellious. He even attacked the Roman Catholic Church for not doing enough for the poverty-stricken. This was another unpopular stand to take. Most Mexicans were Catholic. Their fear of God kept them from challenging the church. (Rivera's father was not Catholic.) His readers

thought no one was supposed to question the church. They found his words outrageous.

To make matters worse, Guanajuato had a new governor who didn't care for Señor Rivera's type of journalism. This governor did not like it when anyone questioned his authority.

María Rivera knew her husband was making dangerous enemies both in government and in the church. Eventually, the stress was too much for her. She decided to take action. She worked out a plan to pack up the children and sneak out of town.

## Mexico City

María grew increasingly frightened for her husband and her family's safety. She waited until her husband went on one of his visits to the country, then she packed up her seven-year-old son and his sister, and set off by train for Mexico City. It was a thrilling trip for young Rivera, who loved trains. Their destination was exciting, too. Mexico City was the largest city in Mexico. Rivera thought they were only going for a short visit. But he soon found out that the plan was for them to remain in Mexico City to live. When Rivera's father returned home from work he found a note from María that said, "Sell the house and follow." María's mind was made up. Her husband quit his job and joined his family in Mexico City. There, he began a new life. It

## Rivera Honors the Value of Vaccinations in His Work

Vaccinations were first developed in 1796, when an English physician named Edward Jenner found a way to prevent a deadly disease called smallpox. He discovered that if a person was injected with a serum containing a tiny amount of cowpox, the person's body would build up a defense against smallpox. Jenner used animals to produce the serum used in the vaccine. Later, scientists developed vaccines for other illnesses.

Forty years after Rivera recovered from his illnesses, he painted a mural in Detroit. The mural told the story of industry and progress. In one scene, he painted a child being vaccinated surrounded by animals, which shows that they are important in the making of vaccines. Behind the boy, scientists are working in a lab, discovering new medicines.

Diego Rivera, *Vaccination*, detail from *Detroit Industry*, north wall, May 1932–March 1933

Diego Rivera, *Olmec Artisans at Work*, detail from panel 1, *Pan American Unity* mural, 1940

turned out to be a wise move. Shortly after leaving, the governor closed *El Demócrata* and arrested the staff. Speaking out against those in power became even more risky. Writers critical of the government were often beaten up or even murdered.

Young Rivera was heartbroken about the move. He missed Guanajuato and his old house. The family's new home was so small that he couldn't have his art room.

In addition, the Riveras lived in a poor part of town that didn't have good sanitation. His neighborhood did not have sewers or running water. During Rivera's early childhood, the average life span in Mexico was only 24 years. One reason was that so many young children died from diseases that were the result of poor sanitation.

Rivera did become very ill. First he came down with scarlet fever, a painful illness that can be very serious. Then he got typhoid, another dangerous disease, which is spread by infected water or milk. He was so ill that he didn't draw for a year.

Gradually, as Rivera's illness subsided and his health improved, so did the fortunes of his family. His father found a low-paying desk job at the Department of Health. His mother, who had become a midwife, opened up a women's clinic. And young Rivera discovered art school.

## Training to Be an Artist

When Rivera was nine years old, he knew that he wanted to be a professional artist. He persuaded his mother to enroll him in evening art classes at the San Carlos Academy. It was one of the best art schools in Mexico, and he became one of its most talented students.

Rivera was a very bright student. During the day he attended his regular school, where he progressed more quickly than other students. At night, he studied art. When he was 11, he enrolled as a full-time student at the San Carlos Academy. He was much younger than most of his classmates, but he soon outpaced them all.

Because Rivera was such a talented student, he was admitted into classes taught by some of Mexico's greatest artists. Santiago Rebull taught him the basics of drawing and painting. Rebull was a great painter, and had once been a pupil of Ingres. Ingres, who was French, was the most celebrated artist of his time.

Another of Rivera's teachers was José María Velasco. Velasco was famous for his incredible paintings of the Mexican landscape. From him Rivera learned the laws of perspective—how to make his work look three-dimensional.

But it was his teacher Felix Parra who introduced a whole new world of art to Rivera, the artwork of Mexico's past. Before Spain invaded Mexico in the 1500s, the native people had produced a wealth of artwork. This time in the history of Mexican art is called pre-Columbian, because it was before Christopher Columbus came to the New World. Parra researched art from this time period. He shared his enthusiasm for its beauty and meaning with Rivera.

Parra taught Rivera the art of the ancient Mayans, who lived in southern Mexico from about A.D. 300 to 1500. These incredible artists built pyramids and temples. They decorated their walls with brightly colored murals. The Olmecs were an even more ancient group. They lived in the area of Mexico's Gulf Coast as early as 1300 B.C. The Olmecs made beautiful stone sculptures. Some Olmecs tattooed their bodies with images such as jaguars. The Aztecs were great artisans, too. Living in central Mexico from A.D. 1370 to 1521, they were the people who founded Mexico City.

Pre-Columbian art became a lifelong interest for Rivera. One day he would build a museum to house the beautiful pieces he collected. (See chapter 8 for details.)

## Skeletons and Folktales

There was another artist who greatly influenced Rivera. He was not an instructor at the academy, but later Rivera called him his greatest teacher.

Posada used several techniques to make his prints. In his early years, he made them by drawing a design on a metal plate, using a very sharp pointed tool. When ink was applied to the plate, it didn't collect in the indentations. A sheet of paper was pressed onto the plate by a machine called a press. When the paper was lifted, the image appeared on it in reverse. If the paper was white, Posada's design would appear as white lines, where the ink didn't print. Posada could make many copies of the same design. He simply re-inked the plate as he pressed new sheets of paper. This process is called engraving.

Later, Posada found a quicker way to make his drawings. Using a pen filled with special, greasy ink, he drew a picture on a plate made of zinc. Then he placed the plate in an acid bath. The acid cut into the plate everywhere it wasn't protected by the grease. When he applied ink to the plate, it collected on the raised area that was his design. If the ink was black, Posada's printed design appeared as black lines. This process is called etching. Posada liked to print his etchings on brightly colored paper.

José Guadalupe Posada, *La Calavera Catrina*, c. 1910

His name was José Guadalupe Posada and he was an engraver. In his engravings, he portrayed scenes of life in Mexico. (For more on engraving see the sidebar on this page.)

Posada's shop was near the San Carlos Academy, and Rivera walked past it every day on his way to class. Rivera stood at the shop window many times. He loved watching the artist work. One day Posada invited him inside.

Posada showed Rivera his etchings of ordinary people living, working, and celebrating holidays. He explained how he used his art to express his opinion about current events in Mexican politics. And he loved to add skeletons. The type of skeleton Posada drew is called a *calavera*. It is a symbol for a holiday called the Day of the Dead. In Spanish, this holiday is called *el Día de los Muertos* (el DEE-ah day lohs MWIAR-tohs). Celebrated throughout

Mexico, it's a holiday that honors ancestors and friends who have died.

Posada had another trademark, too. Often he would etch the words of Mexican folk songs or folktales below his drawings. They were songs that everyone knew.

The artist sold his etchings for pennies. He printed them on inexpensive paper so that his art would be affordable for everyone. The townspeople loved them. Even the poorest people bought them. Later in his life, Rivera would remember how important it was that everyone was able to see Posada's art and learn his message. Many years later Rivera realized how much of what he saw in Posada's studio influenced his own art. It was the art of common people, and it had a message.

## Dreams Across the Ocean

Rivera was busy studying at the academy when he met another influential Mexican artist. His real name was Gerardo Murillo but he called himself Dr. Atl (a-tel). Atl had just returned from Europe, and he was convinced that artists who wanted to create true art could only learn to do so there. In France, students could go to a museum, such as the Louvre, and see great works of art. Throughout Europe, an artist could study the works of masters such as Michelangelo (1475–1564), who painted incredible murals in Italy, and Diego Velázquez

# Activity  Posada Printing

**Posada is famous for his engravings of calaveras—especially a character known as Catrina. Posada designed Catrina as a way to poke fun at overdressed wealthy Mexican women who had a passion for everything French. In his artwork, he dresses Catrina in the elaborate feathered hats and bustled gowns that were popular at the time. Design a character and print your own personalized stationery, invitations, or stickers.**

## Materials

Drawing paper

Pencil

Styrofoam plate

Scissors

Pen

Permanent marker

Toothpick

Paper

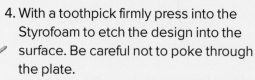

1. Using a pencil, draw a small, simple picture on a piece of paper. It can be a stylized person, a logo, a Posada-inspired skeleton—anything you like.

2. Cut the raised outer rim from the Styrofoam plate. Discard the rim—you'll use only the remaining flat surface.

3. With a pen redraw your design onto the trimmed Styrofoam plate.

4. With a toothpick firmly press into the Styrofoam to etch the design into the surface. Be careful not to poke through the plate.

5. Ink the plate with a marker, gently running it back and forth over the design. The engraved lines will not fill with ink.

6. Place a piece of paper on top of the inked area. Try not to move the paper once you've put it over the inked area.

7. Use the base of the marker to rub back and forth over the paper. Press hard. Lift the paper to see your design.

8. Re-ink the plate and repeat for more copies.

**11**

## The Day(s) of the Dead

Every year on November 1 and 2, playful skeletons come out to celebrate *los Días de los Muertos*. This two-day celebration is a blend of ancient Indian traditions and Catholic customs, but it's also uniquely Mexican.

The holiday begins on November 1. In some ways it's like Halloween. At the market, vendors sell sugary skull-shaped candies. Pictures of playful-looking calaveras and ghosts appear everywhere. Young people go trick-or-treating, saying *"Me da mi calaverita?"* ("Won't you cooperate with the skull?")

On the morning of November 2, families picnic at the cemetery. This may seem an odd place to have a picnic, but it's perfect for the Day of the Dead. Long ago, native Mexicans believed that the dead returned once a year on this day to be fed. It's a happy occasion. First, the family gathers at the grave of a relative. They clean the grave, plant some flowers, and say prayers. If their relative had a favorite song, they sing it for him or her. All the visitors do their part to bring a little cheer to the spirit of the departed.

(1599–1660), who was once the Spanish king's court painter.

The famous artists of the day, such as Claude Monet and Paul Cézanne, lived in Europe. An aspiring student could actually meet these artists and learn from them firsthand. After eight years at the academy, Rivera graduated with honors. And after meeting Dr. Atl, he knew where he needed to go to continue his art studies.

But first he had to find a way to get there. There are many legends about how this happened. One is that Rivera's father set off for Veracruz on business, taking Rivera along to sketch the landscape. Rivera claimed that Teodoro Dehesa, the governor of Veracruz, one day noticed him sketching near his office. Dehesa was in charge of giving scholarships to artists. "My boy," said Dehesa, "you have great talent. You must go to Europe."

The truth seems to be that critics and officials had told Dehesa about Rivera. They had recommended Rivera for the scholarship. Dehesa visited the San Carlos Academy and saw Rivera's work at an exhibition.

Either way, Dehesa was extremely impressed. He offered Rivera a scholarship to study in Europe. The money came from the state treasury and went toward Rivera's living expenses.

But the scholarship came with two conditions. The first requirement was that Rivera had to send Dehesa one painting every six months. In this way the governor would be able to see Rivera's progress. Second, Rivera had to pay his own way to get to Europe. This was quite a challenge for the 19-year-old artist. But Rivera was determined!

He gathered his best paintings and held two exhibits. The shows were successful, and his paintings sold. He was able to purchase a one-way ticket on a steamship to Spain. Rivera was on his way.

## The Mexican Cowboy

The year was 1907. Rivera was 20 years old. Rivera arrived in Madrid, Spain, on January 6. He had a short curly beard, and his wild hair was tucked under his favorite hat. Because of this hat, a Stetson cowboy hat, everyone called him the Mexican Cowboy. But most people didn't notice such small details when they first met him. That's because he stood more than six feet tall and weighed almost 300 pounds. Like his father, he had grown into a mountain of a man, and he made quite an impression.

Meanwhile, back in Mexico, another event was taking place. On July 6, 1907, at 8:30 in the morning, a baby girl was born. Someday her path would cross Rivera's. Her name was Frida Kahlo.

# Activity  Calavera Creations

While Halloween skeletons are supposed to be spooky, Day of the Dead calaveras tickle the funny bone. Make a calavera with its own playful personality.

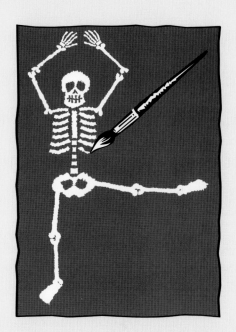

## Materials

Black construction paper

Pencil

White paint

Paintbrush

White glue

Decorative materials such as sequins, feathers, fabric, colored paper, and tissue paper

1. Decide how your calavera will pose and what it will wear. Perhaps it will wear a baseball cap, hold a bag of popcorn, and kick a soccer ball. Or maybe it will dress in a tutu and ballet slippers, and hold a rose.

2. Using a pencil, sketch a basic skeleton shape on black construction paper. Be sure to position the bones in a way that suits your design.

3. Paint the bones white and let your work dry.

4. Add decorations to give your calavera personality. A feather glued to its skull, a tutu made of tissue paper, or a costume made of cut paper and sequins are a few ideas.

Kahlo painting *The Two Fridas*, 1939.
Photograph by Nickolas Muray

# 2 Frida Kahlo
# Bright and Full of Mischief

Frida Kahlo was born on July 6, 1907, in Coyoacán (koh-yoh-ah-KAHN), a lovely town with beautiful houses. Cobblestone streets connected parks and gardens to a charming central plaza. Three years earlier, her father had built the family home, which became known as the Casa Azul. It was designed in the shape of the letter *U*. There was a patio in the center, and all the rooms looked out onto the garden. A tall wall separated the patio from the street. At that time, Coyoacán was about one hour's drive from Mexico City. Today it's actually part of the metropolis, or urban area.

Following Mexican tradition, Kahlo's parents gave her a very long name, Magdalena Carmen Frida Kahlo y Calderón. But everyone called her Frida, which means "peace" in German. German was her father's native language.

Kahlo was a round little girl with a dimple in her chin. She had eyebrows that met in the center just like her European grandmother's. Her father, Wilhelm, grew up in Germany. His Hungarian-Jewish parents had immigrated there before his birth. When Wilhelm was a young man studying at the university, his mother died. At about the same time Wilhelm had an accident, a brain injury that caused epileptic seizures. Because of the seizures, Wilhelm decided to give up his studies.

When his father married again (to a woman Wilhelm did not like), Wilhelm decided to travel. His father paid for his passage and wished him luck. Wilhelm was 19 when he boarded a steamship bound for Mexico.

Wilhelm Kahlo made Mexico his home. He never returned to Germany. From the day he arrived in Mexico he called himself Guillermo (gi-YER-mo), which is Wilhelm in Spanish. Three years later, he married a Mexican woman and started a family. His wife died while giving birth to their second child, and Guillermo became a widower with two small children. Then he met Matilde.

Matilde was a *mestizo*, a person of mixed European and American Indian ancestry. Her father was native Mexican and her mother was Spanish. Like many girls at the time, Matilde never went to school, and she didn't know how to read or write. She married Guillermo and they had four daughters. Frida was the third.

Matilde was very strict with her daughters. Frida, who wasn't always respectful, called her *el jefe* ("the chief") behind her back.

Kahlo's mother taught her children all the things young girls in Mexico needed to know. They learned how to sew, cook, and clean before they entered kindergarten. Matilde thought these were important skills to learn. It didn't matter that the family had

housekeepers to do many of these chores. It was a tradition. She also taught her daughters the art of embroidery.

Matilde was a devout Catholic, and wanted to' bring up her children to be the same. Their church was only a few blocks away from the Casa Azul, and every day they walked to the church to pray. Passing the beautiful plaza, they entered their ornate church. In the dark interior, Frida saw the flicker of flames from votive candles, and she smelled their burning wax. People lit these candles for special prayers. Frida also saw tiny metal charms dangling from fabric panels near statues of saints. When someone needed a miraculous cure, he or she would pin a charm, called a *milagro* (Spanish for "miracle"), onto the fabric and say a prayer. The milagro was usually shaped like a body part (arm, heart, or leg). It represented the body part that needed healing. For example, a milagro in the shape of an arm might be used for someone who had a broken wrist. Churchgoers also set little paintings, called *retablos*, in the church. They made these themselves to give thanks for a miracle. All her life, Frida loved these small folk paintings. Every Sunday, Matilde and the girls attended mass, always sitting on the same bench. Later, when Kahlo became a painter, her art was influenced by these experiences.

The Kahlo children were expected to be devout at home, too. Before each meal, they were supposed to pray. But young Frida was full of mischief. She and her younger sister Cristina would peek at each other across the table and try not to giggle. Despite their mother's warnings, they often played hooky instead of attending their catechism classes. The classes were intended to teach Catholic children religious lessons. Eventually, on a special Sunday, the children would celebrate together in an important church service called First Communion. Sometimes Frida and her sister hid in a nearby orchard during the time they were supposed to be preparing for their First Communion.

### Papa's Little Girl

Because she was so free-spirited, Frida did not get along very well with her mother. But she was her father's favorite. In fact, he once declared that "Frida is the most like me." Guillermo was a professional photographer, and he often took his favorite daughter with him on assignments. In recognition of his talents, the government hired him to photograph Mexico's beautiful buildings and monuments. His photographs were later published as a book.

Guillermo Kahlo was also an amateur painter. On Sundays, he took his daughter with him when he worked on his watercolors. While her father painted at the nearby river, Frida explored its banks. She collected interesting stones, plants, and even insects. Back at home, they examined her treasures under a microscope. She and her father shared an excitement about nature.

But Frida's adventures with her father weren't always fun. Sometimes she had to take care of him. Because Guillermo was an epileptic, he sometimes had violent seizures. During a seizure, he would fall down and become disoriented. It was Frida's job to help him. She knew just what to do. To revive him, she had him smell strong medicine that she carried with her. If he had a seizure while out taking photographs, Frida watched to make sure no one stole his camera. It would be a disaster if it were stolen because they couldn't afford to buy another one.

## The Fairy Tale Ends

When Frida was six years old, she woke up one morning with terrible pains in her right leg. The doctor soon concluded that she had polio, an infectious disease that damages the nervous system and often causes paralysis. As a result, the muscles in her right leg stopped growing. Along with the pain, her right leg became thinner and shorter than her left. But worst of all, because of the doctor's fear that she might infect someone else, Kahlo had to stay inside her home for nine months. She could no longer play with her friends or take walks with her father.

But Kahlo had a secret weapon—her imagination. During her illness, she dwelled in her own make-believe world. She invented a secret friend. To visit her, she fogged up her bedroom window with her breath. She drew a door in the mist with her finger, and imagined flying right through it and into the village. When she spotted a nearby dairy called Pinzón, she flew through the letter *O* in its sign. There she entered her secret world and met her imaginary friend. This friend was always happy. She laughed a lot and danced as if she weighed nothing at all. She always listened to Kahlo's problems and cheered her up.

Luckily, Kahlo wasn't left permanently paralyzed by polio. As she recovered, her father encouraged her to exercise her leg. She swam, played soccer, and wrestled. She enjoyed sports that most respectable girls didn't play. In Kahlo's day, little girls were expected to wear ruffled dresses and play with dolls. But not Frida. She dressed like a tomboy. She loved to ride up and down the street on her bicycle.

Even with exercise, Kahlo's right leg remained smaller than her left. At school, some of the children teased her by calling her "Frida *pata de palo!*" ("Frida peg leg!") She responded with furious curses at them. "At first I assumed that the children's taunts wouldn't affect me," she remembered, "but

José Guadalupe Posada, *Gran calavera eléctrica* ("Big trolley calavera"), 1907
**Electric trolleys were well known for the accidents they caused. Posada made many etchings about this type of tragedy. Here, he shows a cemetery crowded with victims of trolley accidents.**

later they really did, and each time worse." To hide her thin leg she wore extra socks, and a slightly raised right shoe.

Kahlo's disability didn't stop her from having fun. After school, she and her friends had great adventures exploring Coyoacán. They played on the lush, grassy banks of the river that snaked through the village. They skipped in the plaza, past organ-grinders and street vendors selling delicious treats such as *churros* (long doughnuts). The girls knew the names of all the vendors.

## La Prepa

Although Kahlo didn't always get along with her teachers, she was a brilliant student. As she got older, her father realized that the local school wasn't challenging her enough. When she turned 15, he enrolled her in the National Preparatory School in Mexico City.

The school, called La Prepa for short, was considered the best school in Mexico. Tuition was free, and only the brightest students were accepted. When Kahlo applied, she had to take a difficult entrance exam. She scored very well and entered La Prepa in 1922. At the time, girls were discouraged from going to school with boys. As a result, Kahlo was one of only 35 girls in a class of about 2,000. As adults, some of her classmates would become leaders who made great changes in Mexico. As for Kahlo, she wanted to become a doctor.

To get to her new school, Kahlo rode a trolley into the heart of Mexico City. It was powered by an overhead electric cable, and ran on rails laid into the streets. The ride took an hour, but once she got there Kahlo was thrilled! Her school was located near the central plaza and the National Palace, which housed Mexico's government offices. This area, called the *Zócalo*, has a tremendous history. Before the Spanish conquered Mexico, it was a great square where more than 70 Aztec temples, schools, and palaces stood.

When Kahlo first arrived at La Prepa, she looked like a German schoolgirl. The school didn't require uniforms, but her white blouse, big tie, and navy-blue pleated skirt looked like one. To top it off, she wore a straw hat decorated with ribbons that hung down the back. She still walked with a limp, but by now she had learned to cope with it. Her new friends thought this made her more exotic. Kahlo enjoyed appearing mysterious. Soon, she abandoned her schoolgirl look for more unusual fashions. She liked to wear men's suits or dramatic dresses she designed herself.

Kahlo always carried a knapsack. In it were textbooks, notebooks, drawings, dead butterflies, dried flowers, and crayons. For fun, she drew sketches of herself and others. She took art classes but considered her artwork just a hobby. The school required students to take one course in drawing and another in clay modeling.

Although Kahlo was a bright student, she wasn't diligent. Her favorite activity at school was talking with her friends. Before class she often spent time with a group who called themselves the *Contemporáneos* (meaning "contemporaries"). They liked to discuss books, and some of them later became well-known poets. Another group

called themselves the *Maistros*. (The word *maestro* means professor or master. The word is often used playfully.) They liked to discuss politics; everyone had ideas about how Mexico should be governed. But the group Kahlo liked the most called themselves the *Cachuchas*, named after the red caps they wore. This group included the most ambitious and rebellious students.

The seven boys and two girls who comprised the Cachuchas were known for their bright minds, as well as their devilish pranks. Once they rode a donkey through the hallways of the school. Kahlo was so mischievous, the principal tried to expel her. Instead of showing remorse, Kahlo went straight to the minister of education, the principal's boss. With an innocent face, she politely asked to be let back into the school. When he saw Kahlo's high grades the minister told the principal, "If you can't manage a little girl like that, you are not fit to be director of such an institution."

The Cachuchas liked to meet in the library, where they did their schoolwork. But the library wasn't a quiet place when they were around. They teased each other, argued, and planned how to change the Mexican government. They also had contests to see who could discover the most interesting book, and then who could finish reading it first. Sometimes, they acted out what

# The Mexican Renaissance

The word *renaissance* comes from a Latin word that means "to be born again." That's just what happened in Mexico after the Revolution. Artists sprang back to life; they created murals, paintings, and photographs that were purely Mexican. Other creative people, such as architects, writers, musicians, and dancers, joined this Renaissance as well.

Before the revolution, Porfirio Díaz was the dictator of Mexico. During his rule, people followed European ideas of art and culture. Most people looked down on native Mexican culture. "Sophisticated" Mexicans wore clothes designed in Paris and decorated their homes with French furniture. Those who could afford it enjoyed Italian operas at an opera house built of Italian marble. They collected paintings by European artists. The most talented Mexican art students, such as Rivera, got scholarships to study in Europe and refine their skills. Díaz, who had the bronze skin of his native ancestors, went so far as to use powder to lighten his complexion. He did this so that he would look more European.

After the Revolution, which lasted 10 years, everything changed. Mexico was finally Mexican! Rivera and other artists left Europe and came home. The Renaissance had begun. All types of artists began to look to their native heritage for inspiration. Kahlo was influenced by her country's folk art. Carlos Chávez, a famous composer, wove Mexican folk songs into his classical music. And photographers such as Lola Alvarez Bravo captured scenes that were truly Mexican. In a new style of modern dance, artists incorporated into their performances movements such as grinding corn and holding a baby in a shawl. These common activities, the ordinary movements of Mexican women, were celebrated through dance.

they read. Each of them could read at least one foreign language. Kahlo could read three languages: Spanish, English, and German.

## Kahlo Meets an Artist

While Kahlo was in high school, Mexico was going through exciting changes. The Mexican Revolution had just ended and new leaders were creating policies to improve the country. The minister of education, José Vasconcelos, had a big role in these changes. He was in charge of bringing education to all the people of Mexico, rich and poor alike. To do his, he encouraged new programs in literacy. He made it a requirement that art be taught in all the schools. Also, he wanted Mexicans to learn about their rich history. He thought that painting historic scenes on the walls of public buildings, such as the National Preparatory School, would be a wonderful way to tell Mexico's story. He hired many artists to paint these murals. One was a brilliant painter who had just returned from studying art in Europe, Diego Rivera.

In the auditorium of La Prepa, Diego Rivera, then 36 years old, was painting his first mural. In Rivera's autobiography *My Art, My Life,* he described his first encounter with a person who would have a huge effect on his life. He was painting high on a scaffold when "all of a sudden the door flew open, and a girl who seemed to be no more than ten or twelve was propelled inside . . ." he remembered. "She had unusual dignity and self-assurance, and there was a strange fire in her eyes."

The girl was 16-year-old Frida Kahlo. "Would it cause you any annoyance if I watched you at work?" she asked. "No, young lady, I'd be charmed," Rivera replied.

Kahlo sat down and watched him silently, her eyes riveted on every move of his paintbrush. After a few hours, Rivera's wife, Lupe, became jealous and started insulting her. Kahlo merely stiffened and returned Lupe's stare without a word.

Rivera's story is most likely an exaggeration. But Kahlo's friends were shocked when she announced her crush on the artist. They thought Rivera was too ugly, too old, *and* he was married! In the following months, Kahlo watched Rivera's mural come to life. To get his attention, she constantly played tricks on him. She'd steal food from his lunch basket when he wasn't looking, and hide behind the pillars of the auditorium, calling out to tease him. Playfully, she called him *Panzón* ("fat belly"). To Rivera, she was just a little school girl, an annoyance.

Kahlo's crush didn't last long. Someone else caught her attention. He was her classmate, and leader of the Cachuchas, Alejandro (Alex) Gómez Arias. Arias was handsome and charming, and Kahlo called him her *novio* ("boyfriend"). She forgot all about Rivera.

Rivera painting a fresco, 1932

For three years Kahlo and Alex saw each other as much as possible. Young women were not supposed to go on dates alone in those days, so Kahlo made up excuses to meet him. For example, she lied to her mother about having to take an exam at school on a day when there were no classes. That way she could spend the entire day in Mexico City with Alex. They often spent time riding the city buses together.

## An Artist's Apprentice

Schoolwork and romance weren't Kahlo's only concerns. Because of changes in the government, her father's photography business was slow. Under Díaz he had been hired to photograph Mexico's beautiful buildings. When Díaz was thrown out of office, this assignment ended. As a result, Kahlo had to take on part-time jobs to help support her family while attending school. She worked as a cashier at a drugstore, but she wasn't good at counting change. At the end of each shift, when she totaled up the money in the cash register, she often had to add her own money to make it balance. Her jobs didn't last long. She kept accounts for a lumberyard, worked in a library, and had a job at a factory.

Then her father found her the perfect job. He had a friend who owned a print shop. The owner was looking for an apprentice to train in the art of engraving. Frida's father had already taught her how to retouch and color black-and-white photos. Using a small brush and careful strokes, she had occasionally helped him with this part of his photography business. She also learned how to use a camera and develop photographs. Engraving was something she could definitely learn to do.

Fernando Fernández, the owner of the print shop, began by teaching Kahlo how to draw. Her assignment was to copy the prints of an Impressionist artist named Anders Zorn. When Fernández looked at Kahlo's pen-and-ink sketches he realized that she had enormous talent.

## A Day That Changed Everything

On a rainy September afternoon, Kahlo and Arias were riding home from school on a brightly colored wooden bus. As it rounded a corner it collided with a slow-moving trolley. The initial collision was minor. But the trolley didn't stop. It crushed people who fell beneath it. Finally, it pushed the bus against a wall until the bus shattered. Arias was thrown under the trolley. Its three cars passed above him and left him, miraculously, unhurt. But when he got up and looked around, he saw that others had not been so lucky.

He found Kahlo lying in the street. She was bathed in blood but still alive. Kahlo's body had

22

been pierced by a metal handrail from the trolley. A panicked bystander insisted that they should pull the metal shaft out. Arias watched as the stranger put his knee on Kahlo's body and yanked out the piece of metal. Kahlo's screams, Arias later said, "were louder than the ambulance's siren." Gently, he picked her up and placed her on a billiard table at a nearby pool hall. He covered her with his coat and stayed with her until an ambulance came. Believing Kahlo was beyond saving, the ambulance staff carried others away first.

The doctors expected Kahlo, who was only 18, to die on the operating table. Many of her bones were broken, including her spine, collarbone, ribs, pelvis, and right leg. Her right foot was twisted and crushed. Her most serious injury, though, was caused by the handrail. But Kahlo was lucky. Despite her massive injuries, she survived.

Kahlo stayed in the hospital for a month. To keep her still while her bones healed, the doctors placed her in a full-body cast. She lay flat on her back in a boxlike structure that looked like a coffin. At first, her parents were too upset to visit her. "My mother was speechless for a month," Kahlo remembered. "It made my father so sad that he became ill." Her older sister, Matilde, stayed by Kahlo's side. "It was Matilde who lifted my spirits; she told me jokes. She made everyone in the room howl with laughter."

When the doctors felt Kahlo was ready, they sent her home in a plaster cast that reached from below her neck down to her waist. Called a corset, it kept her spine straight while it continued to heal. Kahlo was confined to bed. She lay flat on her back for three more months. Even worse, she had to drop out of school. Her friends, including Arias, came to visit now and then, but they grew tired of the long ride to Coyoacán. Later, Arias's parents sent him on a nine-month trip to Europe. Some think that Alex's parents sent him abroad to cool off his relationship with Kahlo. Alex, too, may have wanted to get away from her neediness. She wrote him often, begging him to visit, and telling him how much she was suffering. Once again, it was Kahlo's imagination that came to her rescue. This time, though, she used paint to express her hopes and fears.

"Without giving it any particular thought," Kahlo later recalled, "I started painting." Her father lent her his oil paints. Her mother ordered a special lap easel so she could paint lying down. And she attached a mirror above Kahlo, underneath her bed's canopy. This way, Kahlo could be her own model and paint self-portraits.

To learn more, Kahlo pored through art books. As she would later do during her apprenticeship, she practiced by imitating other artists. She copied their painting styles and color choices. Some of her favorites were the Italian Renaissance painters.

# Activity      **Painting Mastery**

**While recovering from her accident, Kahlo spent hours reading art books and gazing at paintings by famous artists. To practice, she tried to copy their styles. Kahlo especially liked the art of Italian Renaissance painters. Make a portrait in a style that _you_ admire.**

### Materials

Art books with pictures by portrait artists

Drawing paper

Pencil

Painting or coloring supplies of your choice

1. Look at several art books to decide which artist and which style you'd like to imitate. Perhaps you admire Leonardo da Vinci's _Mona Lisa_, Vincent van Gogh's self-portraits, or Giuseppe Arcimboldo's faces made of fruit.

2. Study one painting in detail to see how the artist used color, shape, and line. Notice how he or she painted the background. Are the colors bright or subdued? Does the artist include props, such as a book or personal item, to tell viewers something about the subject? What stands out about your chosen artist's work that makes his or her portraits different from those of other artists? Think of how you can include these ideas in your own art.

3. Put a sample of your selected picture next to you while you create a portrait of yourself or a friend. Match the style of your chosen artist by incorporating as many of his or her ideas as possible while painting your chosen subject.

4. Place your finished picture next to the one you selected to see how closely you were able to follow its style.

She gave her first painting of herself to Arias. It was titled _Self-Portrait Wearing a Velvet Dress_. In it she wears an elegant red velvet dress with a gold brocade collar. It resembles the lush fabrics worn by women during the Italian Renaissance. In fact, Kahlo thought her style was a little like that of the famous Italian Renaissance painter Sandro Botticelli. When she wrote to Arias she referred to herself as "your Botticelli." She asked Alex to hang her portrait at a height that would make it seem as if she was in the room with him. That way he wouldn't forget her. She missed him terribly, and hoped the painting would reunite them.

Arias did not forget Kahlo. When he returned from Europe their relationship was strained. Though they remained friends for the rest of their lives, their romance ended. Arias went on to study law and later became a famous speaker.

Over the course of the next two years, Kahlo was able to get up out of bed. She even started to walk. But her health remained poor, and she was often in pain. Determined, Kahlo kept painting. Practicing different styles, she painted portraits of her sister, Adriana, and friends in her neighborhood. Little by little, she tried to improve her skills. She knew her parents were burdened with medical bills, and her father's business was still slow. She gave up the idea of going to medical school, and hoped to earn money with her paintings.

But she needed to know one thing: Were her paintings any good?

## Meeting the Master

Kahlo set out for Mexico City with four of her best paintings under her arm. Her destination was the Ministry of Education building. She knew that the famous Diego Rivera was working on a fresco there. She hadn't seen him since her school days. Back then she'd had fun teasing him. But that was six years ago. Now, at age 21, she was all business.

She found the artist sitting high on a scaffold. "Diego, please come down from there!" she shouted. "I have something important to discuss with you!"

Rivera turned and looked down to see a pretty, petite girl. She had long hair and dark, thick eyebrows that met above her nose. To Rivera, her eyebrows seemed like the wings of a dove, their black arches framing two extraordinary brown eyes. He didn't recognize her.

"Look, I didn't come to flirt with you or anything," Kahlo said. "I came to show you my painting. If it interests you, tell me so. If it doesn't interest you, tell me that too, so I can get to work on something else to help out my parents."

Respectfully, the great painter came down from the scaffold to see the paintings. After looking at each of them in turn, he said, "Look, in the first place, I am very interested in your painting, above all in this portrait of you, which is the most original." With that, he gave her an assignment. "Go home, paint a painting, and next Sunday I will come and see it and tell you what I think."

## The Great Artist

Kahlo knew she could rely on Rivera's judgment. He had become one of Mexico's most respected artists. Rivera knew a great deal about all types of art. During the 14 years he lived in Europe, he had seen work by all the masters.

Diego Rivera, *Self-Portrait*, 1941

# 3  Rivera's Ideas

After landing in Spain in 1907, Diego Rivera made his way to its capital, Madrid. Luckily, he spoke the same language as his European hosts. But the people in Madrid speak a type of Spanish called Castilian. As soon as Rivera opened his mouth it was clear that he was a visitor. Natives of Madrid pronounce the letter *z* with a *th* sound, as in the word *think*. Rivera pronounced it like the English letter *s*. The word *zapato* ("shoe") would be pronounced "tha-pato" in Madrid and "sa-pato" in Mexico.

Madrid was a bustling city full of lovely old churches and impressive public squares filled with statues and fountains. The Royal Palace, home to the king and his family, was there.

The Prado, one of the world's most famous art museums, also was located in Madrid. Rivera visited it often to study works by Spanish masters such as Francisco Goya. Goya was born 140 years before Rivera. In his youth, he had painted pleasant scenes of the upper-class enjoying life. But this changed after he suffered an illness that left him deaf. Goya then focused on darker, more unpleasant themes. These paintings, which Rivera greatly admired, are rich with emotion.

Rivera also admired paintings by another artist who had lived in Spain, El Greco. Born in 1541, El Greco spent most of his life in Toledo, a city near Madrid. Experts often cite one of his paintings, *View of the City of Toledo*, as the greatest landscape in the history of art. Because Toledo was near Madrid, Rivera often painted there—copying the same scenes El Greco had painted.

Rivera took art lessons from one of Spain's leading portrait painters, Eduardo Chicharro. Dr. Atl knew of Chicharro's work and had arranged for Rivera to study with him. Chicharro was soon praising his new student's talents. After six months, he wrote a letter that Rivera happily sent off to Governor Dehesa in Mexico. It said that Rivera "has made much progress, which I do not hesitate to qualify as astonishing. And therefore I am pleased to state that Señor Rivera, my pupil, shows that he has magnificent qualities for the art in which he is engaged, and . . . the qualities of a tireless worker." Proudly, Rivera made a copy of the letter and sent it to his father, too.

Over the next two years, however, Rivera began having doubts about his work. He agreed with his teacher that his technical skills were good. He could easily copy the styles of other famous painters, but something was missing. He felt his paintings weren't original, they didn't have a spirit he could call his own.

Searching for answers, he decided to visit Paris to see the art collection in the Louvre. Artists from all over the world congregated there. Rivera met painters from faraway places such as Russia, the United States, and Japan. They gathered in cafés, and

Paul Cézanne, *Still Life with Curtain and Flowered Pitcher*, c. 1898–99

Rivera found himself conversing in three languages: Spanish, French, and Russian. He soon decided to make this city, a hotbed of innovation, his home. He lived and studied in Paris for the next 10 years.

Rivera loved the Parisian art galleries. They showcased a great variety of works by modern artists. By merely strolling up and down the streets and peering into gallery windows, he could learn what others were doing. Rivera was especially excited when he one day spotted a painting by Paul Cézanne. Many young artists were inspired by Cézanne's brilliantly colored landscapes set in southern France, his homeland. They loved his dazzling still-life canvases of fruit, too. Cézanne's apples and oranges seemed as if they might roll right out of the painting into the viewer's lap. Today, Cézanne is considered the father of modern painting.

Rivera was mesmerized by the Cézanne, and was still pondering the painting when the gallery's owner locked up and left for lunch. When he returned, Rivera was still there. It was obvious that Rivera, dressed in shabby clothes, wasn't there to buy anything. The gallery owner gave him an angry look and went inside. After a while, it started to rain. Rivera, however, remained in front of the window, unable to take his eyes off the masterpiece. Suddenly, the art dealer removed the painting from the window. Rivera thought he did this fearing Rivera was a thief planning to steal the painting.

But soon, the man returned carrying another equally wonderful painting! Rivera stood in the rain all afternoon as the dealer replaced canvas after canvas. To Rivera, it was like a private showing of great artists. He saw works by Cézanne, Matisse, Van Gogh, and Renoir. The shop owner was Ambroise Vollard, a dealer who believed in these artists and helped them become famous.

## Life as a Cubist

Rivera began experimenting with a new kind of art that was sweeping through Paris. It was called cubism. Soon, he became a champion of this novel way of looking at the world.

The two artists who are credited with creating cubism are Pablo Picasso and Georges Braque. This new art form broke all the rules. Many earlier styles of art were unique in some way, but they all had at least one thing in common: each picture was intended to resemble the subject. With a portrait, for instance, everyone could recognize that the picture was of a person. The cubists changed all that. They created paintings that many viewers found very odd. At first, a portrait might seem like a mixed-up puzzle of lines and planes, with dabs of

Diego Rivera, *Zapatista Landscape*, 1915

# *Activity*  **Mixed-Up Masterpiece**

Rivera's cubist painting of Zapata is like a mixed-up puzzle. But the longer we look at it, the more pieces of the puzzle we recognize. Try it out yourself! Combine two pictures to create a mixed-up masterpiece. See if friends can recognize pieces of each image in your picture to solve the puzzle and identify the two pictures.

## Materials

Magazines with colorful images

Ruler

Pencil

Scissors

Construction paper

Glue stick

1. Find two large pictures that relate to the same theme. For example, one picture might be of a tropical butterfly, the other a scene from a rain forest. The pictures do not have to be the same size, but each should be at least 4 inches square.

2. Using a ruler, divide each picture into 1-inch squares. To do this, first mark off the inches across the top of the picture (width), and then measure the picture from top to bottom (length).

3. Lightly draw lines to create squares dividing up the picture.

4. Cut each picture into 1-inch squares. Set aside any pieces that do not measure at least 1 inch.

5. Allowing for a 1-inch border at the top and left side, arrange the squares on a large sheet of construction paper.

6. Mix the squares in any order you like. For example, start with a square from the rain forest picture in the upper left corner. Next, place two squares from the butterfly picture. Perhaps the next square in line is from the rain forest, and so on. Arrange them row by row, from left to right. You don't have to use all the pieces.

7. Glue the pieces to the paper.

8. Trim the construction paper to leave a 1-inch border around your work.

Here's another idea: turn snapshots of your family vacation into a piece of art. Surround a picture of your family with a mosaic of squares cut from vacation photos. (But check with an adult first before cutting these up.)

color. But studying the painting a bit more, the viewer might start to see a face. Suddenly a nose appears here, a mouth there, and maybe an eye, all mixed into the puzzle of geometric shapes. This is what a cubist portrait looks like.

As Rivera explored cubism, he began to develop his own style. While Picasso and others painted in somewhat muted tones, Rivera used bright, bold colors. They were the colors of Mexico: brilliant blues, lush greens, and fiery reds. He also experimented with different materials. For example, he mixed sand into his paint to add texture. Sometimes, Mexican scenes appeared in his paintings, too.

One painting from this period is called *Zapatista Landscape*. Even though it's in the cubist style, you can see elements of Rivera's theme if you look carefully. His painting tells the story of Emiliano Zapata, a folk hero who played an important part in the Mexican Revolution. Zapata's peasant clothes—a colorful serape and sombrero—dominate the picture. In the background, Rivera painted the mountains that surround Mexico City. In the foreground are a rifle and cartridge belt, Zapata's weapons. In the bottom right-hand corner, Rivera included a detail common in Mexican folk paintings. It is a scrap of paper that looks as if it's nailed to the canvas. In folk paintings, the words of this special feature describe the event portrayed and show the artist's name. For some reason, Rivera left his note card blank.

## Rivera Meets the Master

In Paris Rivera lived near Pablo Picasso and thought of him as a hero. After all, Picasso was known to the world as a leader of the modern art movement. But Rivera didn't meet Picasso right away. One day a friend knocked on the door and delivered a message from the great artist. "He sent me to tell you," the messenger said, "that if you don't go to see him he's coming to see you." From these few words, Rivera realized that Picasso had seen his work and had found it worthwhile. He also knew that Picasso was making a little joke. Picasso had the bad reputation of visiting other artist's studios to snoop. Sometimes, he would steal ideas for his own paintings. Picasso was inviting Rivera to snoop on him first . . . or else.

Of course, Rivera immediately went to Picasso's studio. Later, he remembered the thrill of being invited. He felt as if he were about to meet a god.

Picasso was full of excitement. "Will and energy blazed from his round, black eyes," Rivera remembered. Canvases, stacked against walls, filled his studio. One by one, Picasso took Rivera on a tour

## Back at Home: A Revolution Begins

Three years after Rivera arrived in Europe, a revolution erupted in Mexico. When it began in 1910, the Mexican Revolution had several leaders and many different goals. The one thing all the revolutionaries wanted, however, was to remove Porfirio Díaz from power. Throughout Mexico, citizens armed themselves and prepared to overthrow the corrupt dictator. They hoped to achieve a better way of life through their struggles.

One of the best-known revolutionary leaders was Emiliano Zapata. He came from the sugarcane-growing state of Morelos, south of Mexico City. Zapata represented the peasants who had farmed the mountainous countryside for hundreds of years. Díaz had allowed their land to be confiscated and sold to a few wealthy men.

Zapata's followers, known as *Zapatistas*, wanted their land back and were ready to fight for it. They were often so poor they carried their few possessions on their backs. Many didn't even have shoes, but the barefoot volunteers were fierce fighters.

Frida was four years old when a battle erupted outside her home. "I witnessed with my own eyes Zapata's peasants' battle," she recalled. "My mother opened the windows on Allende Street. She gave access to the Zapatistas, seeing to it that the wounded and hungry jumped from the windows of my house into the living room. She cured them and gave them thick tortillas."

Rivera also agreed with Zapata's revolutionary ideas. Today Zapata is remembered as one of Mexico's most beloved leaders.

In 1911, the revolutionaries defeated Díaz. But for the next nine years, the struggle continued. After Díaz was deposed, others vied for power. The Mexican Revolution finally ended in 1920, with the election of Álvaro Obregón. During his presidency, Obregón worked to distribute some land back to the peasants. One of his most important achievements, however, was the development of the nation's school system. He brought this about with the help of José Vasconcelos, the man who later hired Rivera to paint murals.

José Guadalupe Posada, *Genovevo de la O* [a Zapatista], 1910–12

of the paintings. Afterward, they walked to Rivera's studio to see what he had done. Both artists loved to talk about painting. Because Picasso was from Spain, they could discuss their ideas in Spanish.

Rivera and Picasso became good friends. They shared ideas, but continued to paint in their own unique ways. The critics soon recognized the originality of Rivera's bright, vibrant paintings. They stood out from those of other artists. One critic wrote that Rivera "follows his own road ... between a painting by Rivera and one by Picasso there is as much distance as between a mountain and a forest."

By 1916, Rivera was considered one of the best Cubist painters. That year, his paintings were exhibited in the United States. It was the first time his art was displayed there. The exhibit also featured works by Cézanne, Picasso, and van Gogh.

Rivera should have been happy, but he wasn't. He was homesick. Unfortunately, things were not going well for his country. The Mexican Revolution was still going on. Since Díaz had been thrown from power three different men had ruled the country. The current leader, Venustiano Carranza, didn't treat the poor any better than Díaz had.

Rivera thought it was important for the poor to stand up for themselves. He wondered if he might be able to help. Maybe through his paintings he could show ordinary people how important they

# Rivera's Politics

On many nights, after he finished work, Rivera joined other artists and writers in the neighborhood cafés in Madrid and, later, in Paris. They loved to debate about art, literature, world events, and politics. Rivera was an avid reader, and was especially interested in politics.

While living in Spain, Rivera learned about the writings of a German named Karl Marx. Marx wrote about poverty and injustice. Rivera's father was concerned with these issues, too. Ever since Rivera was a small boy, his father had worked to help poverty-stricken Mexicans. Now Rivera shared his father's concerns. When he read Marx's ideas, he thought about how they related to Mexico.

Marx believed that most societies were divided into two groups. One group, the working class, labored in factories and on farms, producing the goods that everyone used. These people, Marx declared, were usually overworked and underpaid. The second group, the ruling class, were the wealthy business owners who hired the workers. They stayed wealthy by paying the workers as little as possible. Eventually, problems arose between the groups because the ruling class, by providing poor wages and terrible working conditions, took advantage of the working class. According to Marx, society would be better off if the population could share wealth, labor, and power equally among themselves. Rivera thought these ideas made sense.

In 1917, Russia experienced the problems Marx wrote about. A group of revolutionaries, led by Vladimir Lenin and Leon Trotsky, rose up against the ruling czar, Nicholas II. Inspired by Marx's writing, Lenin and Trotsky created a new political ideology called Communism.

Rivera and many of his artist friends shared Marx's ideals, and considered themselves Communists.

## Angeline Beloff

While in Paris, Rivera fell in love with a Russian artist named Angeline Beloff. Even though they were never legally married, some consider her his first wife, as they lived together for 10 years and had a child. Rivera's only son was born August 11, 1916. Shortly after Diego Jr.'s first birthday, the child became very ill. Although Rivera's art was critically praised, sales were slow. Living in a cold, damp apartment, with no money for doctors or medicine, Rivera and Beloff could not help their son. He died of influenza when he was only 14 months old.

While living with Beloff, Rivera had an affair with another Russian artist named Marievna Vorobiev. In 1919 she gave birth to a girl she named Marika. Although Rivera never legally acknowledged Marika as his daughter, he often helped with the child's expenses. Marika grew up to become an accomplished dancer.

Rivera's relationship with Beloff ended in 1921 when he returned to Mexico.

were to their country. Once they understood their importance, they would realize their power. This feeling of power, Rivera hoped, would give people the courage to fight against unfair rulers. Rivera thought he could make a difference in Mexico. But first, his style of painting had to change.

Rivera realized that his cubist paintings could not portray a message clearly. First, these paintings were too hard to understand. Only knowledgeable viewers could relate to them. Second, Rivera remembered what Posada had taught him long ago. Posada brought his message to the people by mass-producing cartoons, and selling them at a price everyone could afford. But Rivera painted canvases. It was usually wealthy people who bought them, which meant that the only people who would see the paintings were the members of the upper class. Rivera knew that art that could inspire the common citizen could not be tucked away in an art gallery. It couldn't hang in the homes of the few who could afford paintings. Farmers and workers would never see them. His art would have to be huge, realistic, and displayed in places where everyone could see it—on the walls of schools, libraries, and railroad stations. He must paint murals!

At about this time, a young Mexican artist named David Alfaro Siqueiros was visiting Paris. He had fought in the Mexican Revolution, and he brought Rivera the latest news from home. Rivera learned that many Mexican artists wanted to express political ideas similar to his own through their art. Together, Siqueiros and Rivera planned how to do it. They agreed that they would use the buildings of Mexico for their canvases. Later, this movement was called the Mexican Mural Movement.

Rivera was excited to return to Mexico. But first he had some research to do. To pay for his studies, the Mexican government gave him a small grant. Rivera also sold some of his paintings. With his finances in order, he set off to see art treasures that resembled those he wanted to create. These were frescoes that Italian artists had painted in the 1500s during the period known as the Italian Renaissance.

## Off to Italy

Rivera filled his knapsack with brushes and paint and set off. He traveled throughout Italy—including Florence, Siena, Assisi, and other cities—for 17 months. He spent much of his time in Rome, gazing at the Sistine Chapel.

The Sistine Chapel is located in the Vatican, which is the headquarters of the Catholic Church and the home of the Pope. In 1508, Pope Julius II hired Michelangelo to paint a fresco on the ceiling of the chapel. It took the artist four years to complete his masterpiece. To reach the high ceiling, he and his assistants had to work on a scaffold that rose

60 feet above the floor! That's the height of a five-story building. When completed, the chapel's murals portrayed nine Biblical stories, including the Creation, Adam and Eve, and Noah and the flood.

The murals made a huge impression on Rivera. He saw how powerful this art form could be. He knew that when the chapel was painted, very few people could read. But Michelangelo's paintings made the stories come to life for everyone. Murals, Rivera was convinced, were a powerful means of communication.

Rivera sketched the scenes from the Sistine Chapel over and over again. He wanted to understand all the major technical problems, such as dividing a large space to show many different scenes. He also made note of how fresco artists integrated their work with the existing architecture, incorporating arches, doorways, and ornamental decoration. Rivera eventually mastered this skill. After almost a year and a half, he had made more than 300 sketches of Michelangelo's work. Now he was ready to go home.

# Learning to Create Murals on Wet Plaster

Rivera's studies of Italian frescoes had taught him how to design wonderful scenes. But they hadn't taught him how to create a fresco. Rivera was an expert at painting on canvas. But he needed other skills to create a mural using wet plaster.

First, the plaster had to have the correct mixture of ingredients. The pigments used as paint had to be ground to just the right consistency. Applying the pigments was another challenge. A large wall had to be painted in many sections. Each section was one day's work. As the plaster dried, the colors became lighter. This made matching the sections difficult. The technique didn't allow for erasing. If Rivera made a mistake, the entire section had to be chiseled off and started again the next day.

Rivera faced all of these problems and more when he first started using the fresco method. Other artists in Mexico also wanted to paint frescoes, but no one knew how.

Rivera's first attempt was a disaster. He was hired to create a mural at the Ministry of Education building in Mexico City. In March of 1923, Rivera began working on the fresco with the aid of three assistants, two plasterers, and five laborers. One evening an assistant passed under Rivera's scaffold as he was leaving work. He noticed that "it was shaking as though an earthquake was about to start." Looking up into the darkness, he saw Rivera's huge figure. Rivera was sobbing uncontrollably, and furiously scrapping his entire day's work from the wall. Other assistants had witnessed similar scenes. They realized that Rivera would have a nervous breakdown if they didn't do something soon.

One of the assistants remembered that his father, a housepainter, had developed a technique for making a type of plaster called stucco. The recipe was similar to that used by the Aztecs' ancestors. These artists had painted incredible murals in their temples. Their frescoes had lasted 1,600 years! The assistant thought this information might help Rivera.

After experimenting with his father's recipe, the assistant showed it to Rivera. It worked! Of course Rivera took credit for it, as he did with all discoveries and creations that occurred under his commission. Rivera took credit for discovering "the Aztec secret" when newspaper reporters interviewed him. Over time, Rivera did have to perfect the recipe. He eventually mastered all the skills necessary for making a fresco. As time went by he taught them to others.

# Activity  Fresco Painting

A fresco is a special type of mural made by applying paint to damp plaster. As the plaster dries, the colors bond to it. Because of this process, fresco paintings last a very long time. Make a mini fresco using ingredients from your pantry.

## Materials

- Pencil
- Paper
- Plastic lid, about 5 inches in diameter, such as a large oatmeal box top
- ½ cup flour
- ¼ cup salt
- ¼ cup water
- ½ tablespoon cooking oil
- Mixing bowl
- Watercolors
- Paintbrush
- Container of water
- Yarn

1. Create a design for your fresco. To do this, place the plastic lid over the paper and trace around its edges. Remove the lid. Draw a picture inside the lines. Keep in mind that your image will soak into a damp plasterlike surface. Large shapes without too much detail work best. Set your drawing aside and refer to it when you paint.

2. Create the surface for your fresco by combining flour, salt, water, and oil in a bowl. Mix the ingredients with your hands until smooth.

3. Place the lid top-down, with the rim facing up. Press dough into the lid until it is full. Pat gently until the dough is level with the sides of the rim.

4. Apply your design to the damp mixture using watercolors and a brush. To do this, dip your brush in water and then load it with watercolor pigment. Smoothly brush the paint onto the surface. Clean your brush in water before applying another color. Cover the entire surface with color.

5. Use the pencil to make a hole in the top before your artwork completely dries so that you can hang it. Let it dry before removing it from the lid. Thread a piece of yarn through the hole and tie it in a knot, creating a loop on which to hang your art.

Note: Your paint will dry to the touch overnight, but wait a few days for the flour mixture to harden before hanging it.

# Activity — Fool the Eye

Rivera painted the scaffolding and artists in *The Making of a Fresco*, in a technique called *trompe l'oeil* (trompe loy). It's a French term that means "fool the eye." Trompe l'oeil art fools a viewer into thinking the painted object is real. It looks three-dimensional.

One trick to successful trompe l'oeil is placing your art in a setting where a fake isn't expected. For instance, a picture of a lizard painted directly onto the wall could fool someone into thinking it was real. If the same painted lizard were displayed in a picture frame and hung on the wall, it would fool no one.

Rivera was such a good artist he didn't need tricks. For example, he used trompe l'oeil in *Zapatista Landscape*, for the note he painted that looks like it's nailed to the lower right-hand corner of the painting.

Try out your own trompe l'oeil and see whose eyes you can fool.

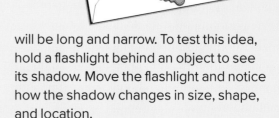

## Materials

- White envelope
- Silver key
- Pencil
- Eraser
- Flash light (optional)

1. Place the envelope so that the flap side faces up. Lay the key on top of the envelope. Trace the shape of the key with a pencil.

2. Color the inside of the key gray. To do this, move the pencil back and forth using very light strokes. Use your finger to blend the strokes into an even tone.

3. Place the real key on the envelope, near your drawing. Notice the details on the real key, such as grooves. Draw a few lines to illustrate these details.

4. Notice that there are highlights on the real key. Erase a few spots of gray to show these highlights.

5. Look for the shadows that the real key throws on the envelope. Add them to your drawing. This is an important part of trompe l'oeil art—objects always cast a shadow. A shadow occurs when an object disrupts a light source. For example, if the setting sun is behind a tree, the tree will cast a shadow on the ground. The size and shape of the shadow depends on the angle of the sun. If the sun is low on the horizon, the shadow will be long and narrow. To test this idea, hold a flashlight behind an object to see its shadow. Move the flashlight and notice how the shadow changes in size, shape, and location.

6. Test it out! Put the envelope on the kitchen table and see who tries to pick up the trompe l'oeil key.

Other ideas: paint a pencil on the cover of a notebook, a bug on a window shade, or a lizard crawling up the wall. Be sure to get permission first.

Diego Rivera, *The Flower Carrier*, 1935

# 4 Mexico, Marriage, and the United States

On 1921, 34-year-old Diego Rivera returned to his homeland full of ideas. He said it was like being reborn. The colors of Mexico energized him. Everywhere he looked, the colors seemed brighter and richer. There were scenes to paint around every corner—in the markets, the fields, and the faces of the people.

The timing for his homecoming was excellent. One year earlier, Mexico had elected a new president, Álvaro Obregón. President Obregón worked to end the Mexican Revolution, and then began rebuilding the country. One important goal was to help Mexico's poor. He gave them land to farm, supported labor reform, and increased their educational opportunities. Most important to Rivera, though, was the president's appointment of José Vasconcelos as the minister of education.

Vasconcelos began by building new schools and public libraries all across Mexico. He thought art should be an important part of Mexican life. With this in mind, he required art education for all schoolchildren.

Vasconcelos invited a group of artists and poets on a trip to the Yucatán Peninsula. The Yucatán was once home to the ancient Mayans. Rivera camped out at the Mayan ruins of Chichén Itzá. He saw pyramids, temples, and shrines. He was fascinated by a fresco in the Temple of the Jaguars. There, 900 years earlier, artists had painted scenes from a battle. Rivera spent hours simply gazing at them. Long after these painters' deaths, their art was still speaking to Rivera.

During the trip, Rivera was able to discuss his ideas with Vasconcelos. He told him of his hopes for painting murals. By the start of the following year, Vasconcelos made arrangements for a mural at the National Preparatory School in Mexico City. It was there, while Rivera was creating the mural (between December 1921 and January 1923) that the young Frida Kahlo teased him with her schoolgirl pranks.

While Rivera worked, other artists gathered to watch. They were intrigued by an art form they hadn't seen before. Some even began to assist him. Before long, many people in Mexico City were talking about the mural.

While painting this mural Rivera also met a woman named Guadalupe Marín. Tall and slim, she soon became his favorite model, and he put her in many of his frescoes. They fell in love and were married while Rivera painted at the school.

As Rivera painted, he realized he was making a mistake with his style. It looked too much like the murals he had seen in Europe. The mural was located at the front of a room that students used for poetry readings, music recitals, and lectures. Vasconcelos had asked Rivera to illustrate a universal theme, and Rivera had chosen "Creation." He filled the mural with 22 figures. Rivera intended these figures to symbolize ideas such as poetry, music,

# Activity    Powerful Pictures and Poems

This activity is based on Rivera's painting *The Flower Carrier*.
Rivera's painting *The Flower Carrier* includes three elements: two people and one very large basket of flowers. The three elements fill up the picture, touching the edges. Does it make you feel a little cramped when you look at it? This tension makes the picture dramatic.

In her book *Still I Rise*, poet Maya Angelou uses Rivera's dramatic images to illustrate her powerful words. Choose a photo and crop it using Rivera's method. Write a poem about the image.

Fast as lightning.
Colorful as a parade.
Happy as Saturday morning.
Touchdown!

## The Picture

### Materials

Magazines or photographs

Pencil

Ruler

Scissors

Gluestick

Writing materials

Construction paper

1. Look through magazines or photographs to find a large picture showing people or animals engaged in an activity. The scene might be of two friends laughing, someone eating an ice cream cone, or a dog curling up and taking a nap. Choose a picture that shows the subject(s) close up. If the scene includes two people and/or animals, they should be right next to one another or even touching. It's fine if other elements surround the picture; you will crop them out.

2. Draw a rectangle on top of the picture to box the figures in your scene. Your lines should touch the figures. Cut the rectangle out.

3. Cut a piece of construction paper that is 2 inches wider and twice as high as your trimmed picture. For example, if your picture is 4 inches wide and 5 inches tall, your paper should measure 6 inches wide and 10 inches tall.

4. Allowing for a 1-inch border at the top and sides of the construction paper, glue the picture to the top half of the paper.

5. Now it's time to add words to your picture. But first take a moment to study the scene. Think about how it makes you feel. Is it a happy scene, or one that is serious, peaceful, or scary? What message does the picture send? For example, a picture of two friends of different races or cultures might send a message about world peace. If the subject in your picture could talk, what would it say?

6. Create a poem that goes along with your picture. For ideas, see the guide on the next page. Write your poem on a piece of paper cut to fit in the area below your picture.

7. Glue the poem onto the construction paper, below the picture.

## The Poem

Follow these steps to write a simple poem.

1. Write three adjectives (words that describe) one under the other. Each word should describe something about your picture. Examples of adjectives are *beautiful, peaceful, cold, crazy, happy,* and *wild.*

2. Combine each adjective with the word *as* followed by a noun (a person, place, or thing) or a phrase. For example: *as ice cream* and *as a bird in flight.*

3. Think of one word that can be the title of your poem. Write this word by itself on the last line.

Here's an example of how this works. For a picture of a football player running with the ball, a poem following this structure is:

Fast as lightning.

Colorful as a parade.

Happy as Saturday morning.

Touchdown!

and knowledge. He painted them in certain poses—thinking viewers would understand his meaning. For example, knowledge appears to be talking while using her hands to make a point. Her pointing hand was supposed to symbolize the idea of knowledge.

When he finished it in 1923, Rivera was unhappy with the result. He realized that using symbols was not an effective way to communicate a message. Many people failed to understand the meaning of his symbols. He knew he had to be more direct, and he wanted to include scenes that were related to Mexico. Although the people in his mural had brown skin and Mexican features, the work didn't portray the *spirit* of Mexico as he intended. Vasconcelos agreed that it was "insufficiently Mexican."

Rivera experienced other problems as well. Despite his study of frescoes in Italy, he had chosen to create this one using a method called *encaustic.* Rivera mistakenly thought this technique would be the most durable. The encaustic method involved painting with pigments that were mixed with beeswax and resin. It was a very slow, tedious process that required assistants to use blowtorches on the walls to keep them warm enough for the wax to bond to the surface of the wall. The mural wasn't his first attempt at the method. He had completed an easel painting in encaustic. But painting a large wall was a much bigger job! He soon realized that the fresco method, although also slow, would be much faster than encaustic.

Rivera learned quite a bit from his first attempt as a muralist. Luckily, there were many more walls waiting to be painted. His next mural, he was determined, would be done in fresco and it would be filled with the spirit of Mexico!

Later that year, Rivera went on another trip sponsored by Vasconcelos. He journeyed to the Isthmus of Tehuantepec, which is located at Mexico's southeastern tip. Once again, he was thrilled with what he found. This time, however, it was the native people that inspired him. They looked and dressed much as their ancestors had 500 years earlier, before the Spaniards arrived. They conveyed just the spirit Rivera was looking for. He drew hundreds of sketches of them. He didn't realize it then, but he would use these sketches in his paintings for the rest of his life.

## Murals with a Message

When he returned to Mexico City in 1923, Rivera began a new mural project. Vasconcelos had commissioned him to paint the walls of the Ministry of Education building, where Vasconcelos had his office. It was an enormous task—and it was perfect for what Rivera had in mind.

Diego Rivera, *Distributing Arms*, c. November 1928

He filled the huge spaces with diverse scenes from Mexican life. He painted people at work farming, mining, and weaving. The mural portrayed the people's enjoyment of life; there were scenes of celebration at weddings and lively fiestas. He painted colorful markets and lush landscapes. He included portraits of famous historical figures, such as Emiliano Zapata.

Rivera hoped his images would inspire the common people of Mexico to realize their power. In a panel he painted a bit later, for example, he portrayed a crowd of poor laborers being handed weapons to use against their oppressors.

Wherever Rivera worked, people came to watch. As his fame grew, artists from all over the world came to learn from him. Because the fresco technique required many talented hands and strong backs, he had several assistants. Some assistants hauled buckets of plaster to spread on the wall's surface. Others ground the pigments that Rivera used as paint. Before all this could be done, carpenters had to build the scaffolding that allowed Rivera to reach the high walls (and sometimes the ceilings) that he painted. Art students often volunteered to do these jobs just to learn from him. Many other artists were painting murals, but Rivera was the master.

Not everyone liked Rivera's murals, however. Because his paintings glorified the poor and often criticized the rich, wealthy people were sometimes offended. Others disliked that many of the Mexicans in Rivera's paintings had dark skin and broad noses. His images were of native Mexicans, not the light-skinned Europeans who were typically seen in popular artwork. Some found Rivera's style too different for their taste. Once, while Rivera was perched high on his scaffold, a man stopped to look at the mural he was working on. He didn't like the way Rivera had painted a particular woman. Rivera overheard this man say to his friend, "How would you like to be married to a woman who looked like that?" To which Rivera shouted down, "Young man, neither would you want to marry a pyramid, but a pyramid is also art."

Some unhappy citizens even tried to destroy the murals they disliked. Fearing the crowd could get violent at any time, Rivera wore a pistol whenever he painted.

Mural painting could be dangerous work in other ways, too. He worked very long hours, at all times of the day and night. Once, while painting a chapel wall at Chapingo, Rivera fell asleep. He fell from his scaffold and landed unconscious on the floor. For three months he had to stay in bed recovering from a fractured skull and severe concussion.

During his recovery, Guadalupe gave birth to their second daughter. They named the baby Ruth.

## Los Tres Grandes

Many artists participated in what became known as the Mexican Mural Movement. Their goal was to beautify buildings while bringing the history of Mexico to the Mexican people. Many of these citizens were poor, uneducated, and illiterate.

The artists shared other goals. They had similar political ideas. They believed that all workers should be paid the same amount of money, regardless of the type of job they held. Because of this, the artists asked for the same wages as housepainters. The artists formed a trade union called the Syndicate of Technical Workers, Painters, and Sculptors.

Three artists in particular stood out. They called themselves *Los Tres Grandes* ("The Three Greats"). One, José Clemente Orozco, was born in Jalisco but moved to Mexico City when he was seven years old. Like Rivera, he studied art at the San Carlos Academy. Another artist, David Alfaro Siqueiros, was born in the city of Chihuahua. He, too, studied at the San Carlos Academy. He was a talented student and a rabble-rouser. In 1911, when Siqueiros was only 15, he led a student strike at the academy. It was designed to force changes in the school's teaching methods. It ended in victory after six months. The academy's director was fired. A new director created classes that were more progressive. One result was the open-air Santa Anita School of Painting.

The third of Los Tres Grandes was Diego Rivera.

## Rufino Tamayo

Not all Mexican painters during this time were involved in the mural movement. Rufino Tamayo had ideas of his own. His fellow artists criticized him harshly. They felt he should be painting politically based nationalistic themes. When the muralists claimed theirs was the only path, Tamayo disagreed. "In art there are millions of paths—as many paths as there are artists," he said. Tamayo thought each artist should have the freedom to explore his or her unique creative journey.

Tamayo was inspired by the modern art of the artists in Europe. He admired the cubist art of Picasso. For color, he found inspiration in a group of artists called the Fauves. They used bold colors that were vibrant but not realistic. He took these styles and others, and combined them with ideas from his Mexican heritage to create his unique artistic vision. He became a celebrated easel painter.

Tamayo was a full-blooded Zapotec Indian, born in the state of Oaxaca in 1899. As a boy, he spent most of his time drawing. Often he went to the National Museum to sit and sketch the archeological treasures of Mexico's past. He was interested in pre-Columbian objects, which influenced his art for the rest of his life. At age 17, he attended a commercial art school and he later became the director of ethnographic drawing at the school. In 1926 he moved to New York, where he spent 10 years teaching at the Brooklyn Museum of Art.

In 1973, he experimented with a new type of printmaking, which used a special type of paper that allowed the ink to soak into it, a process in some ways similar to a fresco painting. The colors are bright and bold. This new graphic process was called *mixographia*.

Tamayo painted murals, too. But like his easel paintings and prints, he preferred themes that did not have political or social messages.

Tamayo is considered one of Mexico's greatest artists. (See the resources section for a Web site featuring his work.)

Diego and Guadalupe's first child, Lupe, had been born two years earlier. While he recovered, Rivera was forced to stay home. But as soon as he was able, he returned to the same punishing work schedule as before. He and Guadalupe grew apart. A year later they got divorced.

## Kahlo Seeks Rivera's Opinion

In 1928, when 21-year-old Frida Kahlo came to show Rivera her paintings, he was already an accomplished artist. In fact, he was famous. When Rivera suggested he visit Frida's home to see more of her artwork, she could hardly believe it.

As he had promised, he showed up the following Sunday. Impressed by the paintings, he told her, "In my opinion, no matter how difficult it is for you, you must continue to paint." He then met her parents and began his courtship. He came to visit her on many more Sundays.

Rivera fell in love with the paintings and the painter. Later, he described his first visit to her home. "When I knocked on the door, I heard someone over my head, whistling 'The Internationale.' In the top of a high tree, I saw Frida in overalls, starting to climb down. Laughing gaily, she took my hand and ushered me through the house, which seemed to be empty, and into her room. Then she paraded all her

# Activity

## Mural with a Social Message

Rivera's murals often focus on social issues. Think of a problem that you'd like to address. How could you use a mural to tell your story? What possible solutions would you include in your picture to help motivate others? Think of your design as having three parts: a problem, a solution, and a result. Paint your message on a large sheet of craft paper that has been taped to a wall.

Here's one example of an environmental message:

**Problem: A scene of a garbage dump polluting the land**

**Solution: People recycling their trash**

**Result: People and animals enjoying an area that would be a dump if they had not recycled**

### Materials

Drawing paper

Pencil

Large blank wall

Roll of craft paper

2-inch-wide masking tape

Poster paint

Paintbrushes

Newspaper

1. Think of a message you'd like to convey in a mural. Decide what you might draw to tell your story. Remember to create your message in three parts: the problem, the solution, and the result.

2. On separate pieces of paper, make a small sketch of each part of your story. Perhaps you have more than one idea for your message. For example, along with recycling, you could show someone using a cloth sack instead of a paper or plastic bag for groceries. Include as many images as you like. Make a small drawing of your mural by combing through the ideas from your sketches. Arrange the parts of your message so that the viewer can easily understand it. To do this, divide the mural into separate scenes.

3. Notice how Rivera divided the different scenes in his murals—he used lines and blocks of color. Use straight or curved lines to separate your scenes. For example, a line might be the branch of a tree or ribbon-like river that flows through the picture. Or you might use different background colors behind each scene to separate one from another. These design elements will make your story flow from one idea to the next.

4. Tape a large sheet of paper on the wall. (Be sure to ask permission first.) To protect the wall, add a strip of masking tape along the top, bottom, and sides of the paper, securing it to the wall.

5. Use a pencil to transfer your sketch onto the wall.

6. Stand back to see how the picture looks. Be sure that the elements in the mural are large enough to see at a distance.

7. Place newspaper on the floor below the picture and paint the mural. Do not paint over the masking tape along the edges of the paper.

## Kahlo's Political Ideas

While at La Prepa, Kahlo became friends with a classmate named Germán de Campo. During her recovery from the trolley accident, he visited her at home. Like Rivera, de Campo was a member of the Communist party. He shared his political ideas with Kahlo. When she was well enough, de Campo took Kahlo to political meetings at the homes of fellow party members. There, people discussed their ideas about Mexico's future. Tina Modotti, who was an accomplished photographer, hosted many of these gatherings. In fact, there is another version of how Kahlo became reacquainted with Rivera that involves Modotti. This version of their second meeting claims that Frida ran into her old panzón at one of Modotti's parties and afterward showed him her paintings.

Many of the people who gathered at Modotti's home were artists. Kahlo met professional painters, photographers, and writers. The parties were lively affairs, filled with dancing, singing, and debate. There were discussions of art as well as politics.

Soon Kahlo joined the Communist Party because she embraced their ideas, too. As a member, she made speeches and marched at protest rallies. These marches were meant to gain attention for issues such as workers' rights. During this time, Kahlo cut her hair very short and often wore red or black long-sleeved work shirts in the style that workers wore. She decorated her shirt with a pin in the shape of a hammer and sickle, a symbol of Russia's Communist Party. Another symbol for Communism was a red star. Rivera paints Kahlo wearing her red shirt, complete with star, in his mural titled *Distributing Arms*.

paintings before me. These, her room, her sparkling presence, filled me with a wonderful joy. I did not know it then, but Frida had already become the most important fact in my life."

The feeling was mutual. Soon they were inseparable. Kahlo spent more and more time on the scaffold, watching Rivera paint. He valued her ideas and began asking her opinion of his work. She thought he was a great painter. But her critiques were not always favorable. When she expressed a negative opinion, Rivera grumbled and carried on. But many times, after expressing his anger, he took her suggestions and made the changes. Kahlo inspired Rivera's work in many ways. For example, she modeled for him. Wearing a man's red work shirt, she hands out rifles and bayonets in Rivera's *Distributing Arms*.

## Marriage

Kahlo and Rivera liked to joke and make fun of themselves and others. Both had quick, imaginative minds. Kahlo still had the wild streak that Rivera had so enjoyed when he first met her. He was flamboyant and, like Kahlo, he loved excitement. They talked for hours about their work, about politics, and about Mexico. Affectionately, Kahlo called Rivera her *Sapo-Rana* ("Toad-Frog"). After a brief courtship, they decided to get married.

Kahlo's father warned Rivera that because of her accident, she would always have health problems. What's more, he warned, she was "a devil." Rivera replied, "I know it!" Señor Kahlo gave permission for them to marry. He knew Kahlo would always have high medical bills. Already, the Kahlos had sold their expensive French furniture and taken in boarders to pay Kahlo's bills. Her father assumed that Rivera would have enough money to pay for the treatments she needed.

Kahlo's mother was not so agreeable. She was appalled that her fiery daughter was about to marry "a fat Communist" twice her age. She refused to attend the wedding. It's likely that she felt better soon after, however, when Rivera paid off the mortgage on the Kahlos' house. Kahlo's parents no longer had to worry about losing their home to the bill collectors.

Actually, Rivera did not have the unlimited funds Kahlo's father had assumed. For a time, he and other muralists in the movement believed in earning housepainters' wages. As Communists they wanted to be part of the working class, not elite artists. After paying for his materials and assistants, Rivera made about $2 a day. Later in his life he accepted higher fees for his mural work. He was also paid well for the canvases he sold to wealthy patrons.

Kahlo's medical bills did grow over the years. Rivera had other expenses, too. He continued to support his children from his previous marriage as well as Kahlo's family. Rivera was a very hard worker. He had to be a salesman as well as an artist. It was financially important for him to have patrons to buy his canvases and to hire him to create murals.

## Kahlo's New Look

Rivera and Kahlo moved into a beautiful house in Mexico City. Happy in her new role, Frida immersed herself in traditional Mexican culture. She decorated their home with colorful folk art that she found in local markets. When Rivera gave her traditional Mexican jewelry and clothing, she stopped wearing modern fashions. She especially liked the style of dress worn by the natives of southern Mexico. The region, called Tehuantepec, had been home to strong, independent women for centuries. Tehuana women wore long, ruffled skirts and colorful, embroidered blouses. They were famous for being the most stately, beautiful, and intelligent women in Mexico.

Kahlo wore these proudly, even though the women around her chose more modern fashions. Her long, dark hair became a work of art, too. She wove colorful yarn into it and pinned it up just as the Tehuana woman did. She wore silver rings, bracelets, and beautiful necklaces like those worn by ancient Aztecs.

Diego Rivera, detail from *Distributing Arms*, c. November 1928

Diego Rivera, *Frida Kahlo*, detail from panel 3, *Pan American Unity* mural, 1940

Her artwork changed too. She no longer tried to match the styles of European painters. She still painted self-portraits but no longer used dark, somber tones. Instead, she used the bright colors of the folk art she collected. Like Rivera, Kahlo loved the colors of Mexico.

## On to America

Meanwhile, the political climate in Mexico was turning against people who held Kahlo and Rivera's views. The government created policies to repress Communist ideas. Speaking out or criticizing the government became dangerous. Some of Kahlo and Rivera's artist friends, such as Siqueiros, were thrown in jail for demonstrating against government policies. Others were deported and even murdered. Bands of racists who called themselves Gold Shirts ran wild, beating up liberals, leftists, and "Indian-lovers." When Rivera left for work each day, he couldn't be certain that he'd return home.

In the United States, a group of art lovers had been trying to persuade Rivera to paint murals there. For years he'd turned them down, preferring to focus on his own country. Now, with the changes in the political climate, it seemed like a good time to leave Mexico. He and Kahlo set off for the United States.

When Kahlo and Rivera arrived in San Francisco, they were celebrities. Patrons who owned Rivera's paintings were thrilled to meet him. With her colorful costumes, Kahlo added exotic excitement. Wealthy hosts threw the couple lavish parties.

Their arrival also caused a flurry of protest. When the public learned that Rivera was hired to paint murals in the city, some complained. Local artists felt that Americans should be hired for such a job, and some people were upset by Rivera's political beliefs.

It didn't take long for Rivera and Kahlo to win them over. Rivera's fun-loving ways and powerful painting, along with Kahlo's exotic looks, captivated America. The famous photographer Edward Weston was a big fan. "I met Rivera!" he wrote. "I stood beside a stone block . . . and he took me clear off my feet in an embrace." About Kahlo, he noted: "Dressed in native costume even to *huaraches* ("leather sandals"), she causes much excitement in the streets of San Francisco. People stop in their tracks to look in wonder."

## A Portrait of the United States

Rivera was thrilled with California! He thought San Francisco was one of the most beautiful cities in the world. He spent weeks touring the area, soaking up the views. From the city's skyscrapers and steel bridges to the countryside's orchards and farmland, Rivera was captivated by what he saw.

Kahlo however, was not so thrilled. She called the United States *Gringolandia. Gringo* comes from a Greek word that means "stranger." But it's used by people in Latin America and Spain as a degrading name for Americans and Britons. This was Kahlo's first trip away from Mexico; she loved San Francisco but was annoyed by the locals' strange ways. She didn't like their bland food, and in fact she thought they were a bit bland themselves. "They all have faces like unbaked rolls, especially the old women," she observed.

There was another reason for Kahlo's bad mood. Her right foot was troubling her. For some reason, it began to turn outward, making it painful to walk. She consulted a doctor, Leo Eloesser, for her pain. He was a friend of Rivera's, and became a lifelong friend to Kahlo. Throughout her life, she kept in touch with Eloesser through letters. She wrote to him often—describing her life, asking for medical advice, and sending affection.

Dr. Eloesser gave Kahlo a thorough physical examination, and discovered that her spine was crooked and lacked one vertebra. It was a condi-tion she had been born with, and it was getting worse. He thought Kahlo's current problems were caused by stress, and recommended that she rest and eat well. It was advice she promptly ignored.

Even though she was homesick and in pain, Kahlo was inspired by California. She wandered through San Francisco, brushing up on her English. She enjoyed riding the cable cars up and down the steep streets, and explored Chinatown in search of Oriental silks, which she turned into long, flowing skirts. She visited museums. And she worked at her own art. Seeing paintings at the art museums must have given her new creative ideas. She was also exposed to the private collections of art owned by Rivera's wealthy patrons.

Eventually, Kahlo had to admit "it did make sense to come here, because it opened my eyes and I have seen an enormous number of new and beautiful things."

Kahlo was especially impressed by the California farms, which produced wonderful fruits, vegetables, and flowers. She thought there was one man responsible for the agricultural abundance she saw: Luther Burbank.

Burbank was born in the east and moved to Santa Rosa, just north of San Francisco, in 1873. For the next 53 years he experimented to develop

## Kahlo's Poor Health

When Kahlo's father warned that she would always have medical problems, he couldn't have imagined just how right he was. After her accident Kahlo was tormented by endless operations. Every new doctor she visited had a different idea about how to treat her. Over the course of her lifetime, she underwent 35 operations. But her numerous treatments and long hospital stays didn't keep her from enjoying life. "It is not worthwhile," she once said, "to leave this world without having had a little fun in life."

Frida Kahlo, *Portrait of Luther Burbank*, 1931

improved, or even entirely new, plants and trees. One way he did this was by attaching branches of one type of fruit tree to the base of a related type of tree. This process is called *grafting*. Because of his discoveries, farmers could grow stronger, more abundant crops, such as the luscious Santa Rosa plum. In fact, because of his experiments with plum trees, prunes (dried plums) became the leading crop in the county for nearly 100 years. Burbank also made the world a more beautiful place. He developed a daisy so big and white that he named it the Shasta Daisy after Mount Shasta, a snow-covered mountain near his home.

While Rivera designed his first San Francisco mural, for the Stock Exchange, Kahlo was hard at work too. Their pictures were very different. Rivera included many of California's riches. Kahlo focused on just one, Luther Burbank. Her portrait of Burbank was unlike anything she had done before.

Kahlo never met Burbank; he died a few years before she came to California. Still, her portrait captures his spirit. He is pictured as part of a tree; his torso is grafted onto its base. His body sprouts from a trunk, whose roots are nourished by a skeleton. Lush leaves grow in his gifted hands.

Kahlo's images sprang from her imagination, as if she saw them in a strange dream. This was the first time she had painted a portrait that was not realistic.

# Activity   Portrait Gone Wild

This activity is based on the Burbank portrait on the facing page. Kahlo's portrait of Luther Burbank does much more than show us what he looked like. It tells a story about who he was and what he did. Use Kahlo's ideas to create a portrait of someone you admire. It can be someone from the past, such as an explorer, scientist, or inventor. Or maybe you'd prefer a famous athlete, artist, or musician. Learn about the person's life and what he or she did to achieve greatness.

## Materials

Several sheets of drawing paper

Pencil

Painting or coloring supplies

1. Make a list of the things you know about your chosen subject. Write down words that describe what they did, when and where they lived, how they dressed, and why they deserve to be remembered today. List things that make your subject stand out. For example, was your subject the first ever to accomplish something? What was your subject's unique contribution? Did your subject influence others who came later?

2. Think of images or symbols that represent the words on your list. On a separate piece of paper, make little sketches of each of these. Draw as many symbols as you can think of (you need not use them all in your final portrait).

3. In pencil, on a separate piece of paper, draw a portrait of your subject.

4. Decide how you can incorporate the symbols into your portrait. Perhaps they spring out of a test tube, are whipped up in a hairdo, flow out of a musical instrument, or are shaped into clouds. If you need to, erase parts of your portrait to integrate the images. You don't have to include all your ideas.

5. Add color to your picture to create a masterful portrait gone wild.

Here's one idea: draw a portrait of Sacagawea (sah-KAH-guh-WEE-uh). Some things you'll learn through research are:

1. She was a Native American, and the only female member of the Lewis and Clark expedition.

2. She was a very valuable guide and interpreter, especially when the group reached the upper Missouri River and the mountains where she had once lived.

3. Some think her English name was Bird Woman.

4. During the expedition, she gave birth to a baby.

Symbols for Sacagawea might include: a bird, a map of the expedition, and mountains. Woven into the portrait might be a bird flowing from her long hair, with a map of the Lewis and Clark expedition decorating the horizon. Instead of legs, Sacagawea's lower body might become part of a mountain range.

## Carlos Chávez

Music also had a role in the Mexican Renaissance. Carlos Chávez was one of the period's finest musicians. He was born near Mexico City in 1899. The youngest of six children, he started taking piano lessons from his brother when he was nine years old. Soon, he began composing his own music. As a young adult, Chávez studied composition at the National Conservatory.

Chávez became one of Mexico's most important composers. He is known for incorporating Mexican folk songs and native instruments into his compositions. In one piece, for example, his score requires traditional Indian drums in the orchestra.

Rivera and Chávez were good friends. In 1929, they decided to put their talents together to create a ballet called *HP* (*Horse Power*). Chávez composed music for the ballet while Rivera designed the dancers' costumes and the sets for the production. Like Chávez's music, Rivera's props were inspired by native Mexican culture. One sketch shows a dancer dressed in a pre-Columbian costume. While Rivera and Kahlo were in New York, fans were thrilled that there would be performances of *HP* in nearby Philadelphia. Leopold Stokowski, one of the most celebrated conductors in the world, would lead the orchestra.

On opening night, Rivera and Kahlo rode to the event in a Pullman railroad car filled with New York's elite. That was how millionaires traveled in those days. Kahlo, in typical fashion, wasn't impressed when she saw the ballet. In a letter to Dr. Eloesser she wrote, "It turned out to be a *porqueria* ["disgusting mess"] . . . not because of the music or the decorations but because of the choreography, since there was a crowd of insipid blonds pretending they were Indians from Tehuantepec. . . ." Clearly, Kahlo would have preferred Mexican ballerinas.

The Americans liked Chávez's music. In 1940, he received a commission to compose a work commemorating an exhibit of Mexican art at New York's Museum of Modern Art (MOMA). The exhibit was titled *20 Centuries of Mexican Art*. Chávez titled his piece *Xochipilli: An Imagined Aztec Music*. In it, four woodwind musicians and six percussionists played native Mexican instruments.

Kahlo was also involved in this MOMA exhibit. One of her paintings, *The Two Fridas*, made up an important part of the show. Chávez and Kahlo were good friends. He believed in her art, and purchased her paintings.

Art historians call this style *surrealism*. Perhaps Kahlo saw surrealist paintings while visiting San Francisco's art museums. If so, they no doubt sparked brand-new ideas. But Kahlo's style of surrealism was completely her own.

## The Story Changes

This visit to America changed Rivera's painting as well. He stopped focusing on the past, as in his Mexican murals, which often portrayed scenes from Mexico's history. In California, Rivera celebrated the present. He titled his Stock Exchange mural *Riches of California*. The mural shows the fruit orchards, gold mines, and shipping docks that were the pride of California.

Before leaving San Francisco, Rivera painted a mural at the California School of Fine Arts. When he first saw the bare wall, Rivera said, "This is too small!" The director of the school found a much bigger wall, which Rivera painted for the same fee.

Rivera intended this mural to inspire the students who would pass by it every day. He titled it *The Making of a Fresco, Showing the Building of a City*. It reveals the excitement of all the building going on in the city. At first glance you notice men and women planning and constructing—hard at work in the building trades. Huge steel beams form skyscrapers, which almost block out an airplane in the sky. Soon, you realize the picture is a mural being painted! Fresco artists are hard at work. Rivera even poked fun at himself. He painted himself in the middle of the picture, back to the viewer, with his plump bottom hanging over the scaffold. Some people didn't find this so funny. A few of his critics saw it as an insult. They decided that by emphasizing his plump bottom Rivera was rudely telling the viewer, "This is what I think of you!"

## An Invitation to Fame

While in California, Rivera received an invitation to create another mural. This one would be in Detroit, home of America's automobile industry. The project was funded by Edsel B. Ford, son of Henry Ford. The theme would be a celebration of industry.

Before Rivera and Kahlo headed for Detroit, they made an important visit to New York City. The Museum of Modern Art (MOMA) wanted to hold an exhibition dedicated entirely to Rivera's

work. This kind of invitation by MOMA signified the height of success for any artist.

Kahlo and Rivera sailed into New York harbor on November 13. Rivera was on deck as the ship docked. Reporters and friends watching from the pier saw the artist waving his arms with excitement as he pointed to the Manhattan skyscrapers, tugboats, and dock workers.

The couple dropped their belongings off at an apartment in the luxurious Hotel Barbizon-Plaza and headed for MOMA. Rivera had a little over a month to get ready for his exhibition. In that time he worked day and night creating new pieces to add to the show. Because he couldn't bring any murals to display, he painted new portable frescoes. He and Kahlo also took time to socialize with the rich and famous. Kahlo met art collectors who would someday buy her paintings. For now, however, Rivera was the star. At the opening of the exhibition, Kahlo stood quietly by his side.

Rivera's exhibition was a tremendous hit! It opened at the end of December 1931 and continued until January 27, 1932. It consisted of 150

pieces, a retrospective of the work he had created during his career thus far. The exhibit included oil paintings, pastels, watercolors, and black-and-white drawings. The stars of the show were eight frescoes, which Rivera had painted on movable panels. These, Rivera created in the month prior to the show. Five of the panels were copies of scenes he had already painted in Mexico. Three were inspired by his observations of New York.

The short notice on this exhibit was because MOMA had just opened. Rivera was only the museum's second one-man exhibit. The first was by the famous French artist Henri Matisse. Rivera's exhibit attracted more visitors than Matisse's. An art critic described Rivera as "the most talked about man on this side of the Atlantic."

In his first year and a half in America, Rivera proved his reputation as a tremendous muralist. Living outside Mexico enabled Kahlo to see new sights and meet new artists and patrons. During this time, her art became more and more imaginative.

Next, the artists moved north, to Detroit. There, Rivera created one of his greatest frescoes.

Diego Rivera, *Production and Manufacture of Engine and Transmission*,
detail from *Detroit Industry*, north wall automotive panel, May 1932–March 1933

# 5 From Detroit to Disaster and Beyond

*D*iego Rivera and Frida Kahlo arrived in Detroit in April 1932 so that Rivera could begin work on a mural celebrating industry. This project was commissioned by Edsel B. Ford. Once again, people treated Kahlo and Rivera like stars. By now their fame had spread across the United States. Many of the well-wishers were Mexicans living in Detroit.

For an entire month, Rivera studied the daily routines at Ford's River Rouge plant in Dearborn, Michigan. He had been fascinated by machinery ever since he was a child. Now, the engineer in him couldn't have been happier, as he watched the assembly line moving parts from one work station to another, each worker performing a specific task. A blast furnace glowed as conveyer belts carried engine parts to be hammered and drilled. Although Rivera didn't know how to drive, he loved watching cars being built.

To study Detroit's other industries, Rivera visited medical laboratories, and workshops that made scientific instruments. In a letter to Dr. Eloesser, Kahlo wrote, "Diego is enchanted with the factories, the machines, etc., like a child with a new toy." But Rivera was even more impressed by the human intelligence and strength behind the machines. He wanted to capture this spirit in his mural.

In fact, the overall mood of Detroit was not all that good. Rivera arrived at the peak of the Great Depression. Many people had lost their jobs. In the automobile industry alone, 311,000 workers had been laid off. Those who managed to keep their jobs at Ford worked for reduced salaries. Their weekly pay was cut by one-third.

Throughout the country, many people could not afford to buy food, much less a new automobile. Ford's assembly line was working at 20 percent of capacity. Corrupt foremen at the factory devised a way to keep earning commissions. They forced workers to buy cars with loans they couldn't afford to repay. In return, these workers were allowed to keep their jobs.

Detroit's wealthy families did not suffer from the Depression as much as lower-income people did. Once again Kahlo and Rivera's patrons wined and dined them.

When it came to politics, the Fords couldn't have been more different from the Riveras. In fact, people like the Fords, who were capitalists, were appalled by the idea of communism. Capitalists believe in private ownership and control of businesses. The Fords were the very type of people Rivera and Kahlo protested against back home. Even so, the Fords found it exciting to know such famous artists. They weren't offended that Rivera and Kahlo disagreed with their lifestyle. Wealthy people like the Fords didn't feel threatened—their riches could not be taken from them. Although they disagreed with Rivera's politics, they found his

## Artists and the Great Depression

On Thursday, October 24, 1929, a crowd gathered outside the New York Stock Exchange and watched as their investments took a nosedive. Known as Black Thursday, it ushered in the beginning of the Great Depression. The collapse had repercussions for the entire world.

Banks went under. When they crashed, the life savings of their customers were gone too. Many people became penniless. Employers had to lay off workers. At the worst of the Depression, 16 million Americans were unemployed. The jobless were everywhere—standing in long lines outside locked factory gates, selling apples on city curbs, and waiting in soup lines. The soup lines were set up by welfare agencies and charities to provide food for thousands of people who would otherwise starve.

The same year Rivera and Kahlo came to Detroit, Franklin D. Roosevelt was elected president of the United States. Immediately, he made reforms. In 1935 he created the Works Progress Administration (WPA) to give jobs to the unemployed. Workers constructed buildings, bridges, and roads. One offshoot of the WPA was the National Youth Administration. It offered high school and college students part-time jobs so they could stay in school.

President Roosevelt didn't forget the artists. Through WPA programs artists created almost 10,000 drawings, paintings, and sculptures. Throughout the United States, they painted murals in public buildings such as post offices. Many of these artists were inspired by the Mexican muralists, especially the works of Diego Rivera.

shocking social messages—just like his personality and his fame—interesting and exciting.

Rivera enjoyed the lavish parties. Kahlo, however, saw the contradiction. Once, she criticized Rivera for dressing like a wealthy capitalist in a fancy tuxedo. Rivera wasn't concerned. "A Communist must dress like the best," he said.

Kahlo was not impressed. She didn't like mingling with these people, and the outrageous side of her personality started to surface. Pretending she couldn't speak English very well, she would throw in foul words when speaking to the prim and proper society ladies who invited her to their tea parties. "What I did to those old biddies!" she would later say, when retelling the story to Rivera. At one fancy gathering, an innocent-looking Kahlo loudly asked Henry Ford, "Are you Jewish?" Everyone in the room, including Kahlo, knew that Ford was anti-Semitic (prejudiced against Jewish people). Kahlo was trying to irritate him. She was famous for being outspoken. Whenever she misbehaved, Rivera would stand to the side and chuckle. He found her outbursts amusing. Henry Ford must have felt the same way; at a later social occasion he asked Kahlo to dance.

Henry Ford was born on a farm in Dearborn, Michigan, in 1863. As a teenager, he enjoyed working on machinery and steam engines. Later, he joined the Edison Company, where his mechanical talent helped him become chief engineer. In his spare time, he tinkered with machinery. His experiments led to an early car that used the same steering mechanism as a boat, a rudder rather than a steering wheel. From this modest beginning Ford created the Ford Motor Company in 1903. He designed an assembly line for building his cars, with workers installing standardized parts.

Rivera admired what Henry Ford had achieved, but he didn't dare praise him too loudly. He later wrote, "I regretted that Henry Ford was a capitalist and one of the richest men on earth. I did not feel free to praise him as long and as loudly as I wanted to." Had Rivera done so, people might have accused him of agreeing with capitalist ideas. Ford tried to give Kahlo one of his big fancy cars (complete with a chauffeur) to use while they were in Detroit. When Rivera and Kahlo refused it as being "too rich for our blood," Ford gave Kahlo a small car to drive herself. All she needed was driving lessons! She had never driven and was thrilled with this opportunity to learn how.

## Celebrating Industry Through Art

With the help of Kahlo—who daily brought his noonday meal along with a large serving of her own artistic advice—and several assistants, Rivera spent nine strenuous months creating his Detroit masterpiece. The work completely absorbed him. He usually spent 15 hours a day on the scaffold, seven days a week.

His workday often started around midnight. That was when his assistant called to announce a section of plaster was ready to be painted. First, Rivera painted the section in outline, filling in with shades of gray—like a black-and-white photo. In that way, he was able to see how the picture looked on the wall.

At sunrise, Rivera reached for the plate his assistant had filled with color pigments. (Rivera used a dinner plate as his palette.) Stroke by stroke, the images sprang to life in brilliant color. He had to work fast to lay down the paint before the plaster dried. When he wasn't happy with his work, his assistants had to chisel off the hardened plaster and start all over. Luckily, this didn't happen very often.

Rivera's finished murals portrayed the story of Detroit's industry, and the people who made it great. The artist believed these murals were his finest work.

## Kahlo "Gleefully Dabbles"

Although Rivera was in the spotlight, some people in Detroit noticed that Kahlo was also an artist. Florence Davies, a reporter for the *Detroit News*, interviewed Kahlo for her column "Girls of

## The Differing Opinions of Ford and Rivera

Rivera and Ford had very different views about how a society should operate. Henry Ford believed in capitalism. In the United States, a capitalist society, Ford was able to take his idea for a car factory and turn it into a successful business. Because Ford was the owner of his company, he was able to keep a large portion of the profits for himself. Ford paid his employees much lower salaries than he paid himself.

On the other hand, if Ford had lived in a communist society, he would not have been allowed to create a factory of his own. In this type of society, the government owns all businesses. Ford would have taken his idea to a government committee. If the government thought it was a good idea, they would create the factory with Ford's help. Ford would not get a large share of the company profits. Instead, the profits would be shared among all employees.

Rivera and Kahlo believed the communist system was fairer. In theory, no one who lived in a communist society would become as wealthy as Ford. On the other hand, neither would anyone be poverty-stricken.

Kahlo loved to be silly. She enjoyed word-play, and mixing expressions from different languages. She made fun of herself as well as others. For example, she had a dark, downy moustache, which you can see in many of her self-portraits. Once at a gathering she announced that it was time for her to go shave.

Everyone had a nickname when Kahlo was around. One friend, Jésus Ríos y Valles, was called *Paisajes* ("Landscapes") because his last name meant "rivers and valleys." She called Rivera's driver General Confusion because he always got lost.

Kahlo could be outrageous, too. She boldly made fun of anyone she thought was arrogant or foolish.

Rivera drawing the cartoon of *Infant in the Bulb of a Plant*, 1932

Yesterday; Visiting Homes of Interesting People." The headline for the article proclaimed "Wife of the Master Mural Painter Gleefully Dabbles in Works of Art." The headline doesn't describe a serious artist. But in the article Davies wrote: "[Frida Kahlo] . . . is a painter in her own right, though very few people know it."

Kahlo painted quite a bit during her stay in Detroit. She took her art seriously, but she pretended it wasn't important. During an interview with Rivera, a reporter once asked Kahlo if she, too, were a painter. With a twinkle in her eye she replied, "Yes, the greatest in the world." At the time, Rivera was the star in the family. But Kahlo's words weren't as outrageous as she thought. Today, the small pieces that she painted in Detroit are better known than Rivera's room-size mural.

Kahlo's choice of materials and technique were different from those of most easel painters. In Detroit, she began painting on sheet metal instead of canvas. This gave her paintings a quality similar to Mexican folk art. Her technique was more like that of a mural painter. Most easel painters start a painting by loosely covering the canvas with color. Instead, Kahlo began by drawing her picture in outlines. Then, starting in the upper left corner, she carefully filled the picture with color. Like a muralist, she worked from the top downward. A muralist begins at the top so that if he or she accidentally drips paint it will not damage an area that has already been painted. The photo-retouching lessons Kahlo had learned from her father showed up in her painting style. Like a retoucher, she used tiny paintbrushes with neat, careful stokes. Kahlo invented her own style of easel too. It was made of a pipe that reached from ceiling to floor. Kahlo attached her artwork to metal pieces that slid up and down along the pipe. This enabled her to adjust the height of the painting as she worked on it. It also enabled her to stand up or sit down while she worked.

While in Detroit, Kahlo experimented with other types of art as well. She and Lucienne tried a style of printmaking called lithography. In *lithography*, an artist uses a grease crayon to draw an image on a flat slab of stone or a sheet of metal. The artist then wets the surface. The area covered with grease repels the water (and remains dry) while the rest of the surface becomes wet. Next, the artist rolls oily ink across the surface. The ink doesn't stick to the wet area, but it does stick to the dry area. In this way, the original image becomes covered with ink. Then the artist presses paper onto the surface to create a print. A lithography expert thought Kahlo's first attempts were "not bad," and could improve with practice. But Kahlo didn't pursue it. She preferred painting.

While in Detroit Kahlo learned that she was pregnant; however, she lost the baby in the fourth month. Doctors had warned her that it would probably be impossible for her to have children because of the trolley accident. This was her second miscarriage, and she was heartbroken. Once again her art helped her overcome her sadness. While still recovering in the hospital, she asked for her paints. Kahlo expressed her disappointment about not having a baby by painting *Henry Ford Hospital*. In this painting she shows herself in a hospital bed. Six objects float around her, linked to her with red ribbons. One of the objects is an unborn baby. Against her doctor's advice, Rivera respected his wife's request and brought reference materials to

Diego Rivera, detail from *Vaccination*, north wall,
*Detroit Industry*, May 1932–March 1933

help her draw the fetus. He knew that creating a picture would be therapeutic for her.

Two months after suffering her miscarriage, Kahlo learned that her mother's health was deteriorating. Kahlo's mother had previously been diagnosed with cancer, but now her condition was much worse. Kahlo and Lucienne Bloch boarded a train back to Mexico. When they arrived at the Mexico City train station, a large group of Kahlo's sisters and cousins were there to meet them. "Everyone was crying and hysterical," Bloch recalled. Kahlo was glad to be with her family, but miserable without Rivera. One week after Kahlo's arrival, her mother died. Kahlo and Bloch returned to Detroit after a six-week visit. A crowd of more than 20 people came to the train station to say good-bye.

While Kahlo was away, Rivera had gone on a crazy diet to lose weight. It consisted of only fruit juice and vegetables. By the time Kahlo returned he had lost a great deal of weight and was nearly unrecognizable. When she got off the train, she couldn't find Rivera, though he was standing right in front of her. "It's me," he called out. Even Rivera had to admit he looked hideous. As he later described it, "My pale flesh hung loosely in elephantine folds." Immediately, Kahlo went to work fattening him back up again.

# Activity   Making It Big!

Rivera was able to enlarge the small sketches for his murals using a grid technique. Often an assistant had the job of making the full-sized enlargement, which is called a cartoon. Lucienne Bloch remembered doing this task in Detroit. She enlarged each one-inch square of Rivera's design to three feet!

## Materials

2 8½-by-11-inch sheets of paper

Ruler

Pencil

1. Cut one piece of 8½-by-11-inch paper in half so that it measures 5½ by 8½. Set one piece aside. You will not use it.

2. Make a line drawing on the 5½-by-8½ paper. (A line drawing uses only lines; it doesn't contain solid or shaded shapes.) You might wish to draw an animal, such as a parrot or horse. Or you might choose a simple scene such as a sailboat on the ocean.

3. Create a grid over your drawing. To do this, start at the left edge of the paper. Lightly draw vertical lines down the page, each line 1 inch from the previous line. Do this across the entire paper. Starting at the top of the paper, measure and draw horizontal lines 1 inch apart. This will create 1-inch squares over your drawing. Set this paper aside.

4. On the 8½-by-11-inch sheet of paper, draw another grid. Make these lines 2 inches apart. This page will have 2-inch squares.

5. Set the two pieces of paper side-by-side. You'll refer to the smaller sheet as you fill in the larger.

6. Starting at the top left square on the larger paper, copy the lines exactly as you see them within the same square on the smaller paper. If there are no lines within a particular square, then go on to an adjoining square. One square at a time, draw the lines as you see them on the smaller page. When complete, you will have an enlargement of your original drawing.

# How to Paint a Fresco

A fresco is a picture painted directly onto fresh plaster before it dries and hardens. As the paint and plaster dry together, the paint becomes permanently bound to the plaster. Rivera was a master fresco painter, but he could never have created his large murals alone. He had many assistants who prepared the walls, made the plaster, ground the pigments used to create the paint, enlarged his drawings, and transferred their outlines onto the walls. (See below for more details on the source of pigments.)

Artists arrived from everywhere, each of them hoping to work with the famous muralist. They worked long hours for very little pay. Rivera didn't pay his assistants much because he didn't have to. He received up to 20 letters a day from all over the world. People wanted to be associated with Rivera. They wanted to learn how to create a fresco.

The plaster was made in the cold basement of the Detroit Institute of Arts. It was a mixture of marble dust, slaked lime, Portland cement, and goat hair. Mixed in huge vats, it had to be beaten with a baseball bat and kneaded with a garden hoe until it was just the right consistency. When it was ready, workers carried it up by a pulley to the scaffolding. They applied four coats of plaster to the walls and allowed them to dry before the final coat, the one on which Rivera painted.

During the preparation of the walls, assistants enlarged Rivera's sketches to the actual size of the mural. Called "cartoons," these enlarged drawings were mere outlines. Rivera drew over the cartoons, adding details. He then pinned the cartoons in position on the wall to see how they would look.

One of the artists who helped with this task was a young woman named Lucienne Bloch. A painter and sculptor, she had spent 10 years in Europe designing glass for a Dutch company. Her father was a respected American composer, Ernest Bloch. When Lucienne Bloch met Rivera, she was on her way to Wisconsin to direct the sculpture department of a school run by renowned architect Frank Lloyd Wright.

Bloch first met Rivera at a banquet in New York during his exhibition at MOMA. She sat next to him, and the two talked excitedly to each other throughout the meal. Kahlo watched them from across the table. She thought Rivera and Bloch were having too much fun together. After dinner, Kahlo confronted Bloch and said "I hate you!" Soon after, Bloch and Kahlo became very good friends. Bloch became one of Rivera's assistants who worked on the Detroit and New York murals; Frank Lloyd Wright had to find another teacher for his school. Bloch remained lifelong friends with both Kahlo and Rivera.

After the cartoons were finished, Rivera and his assistants perforated them with a tool that looks like a pizza cutter, with little spikes around its wheel. The outlined drawing became a pattern of little holes. Before applying the last layer of plaster, the artist pinned the panels in place to the wall. Assistants filled a small muslin or cheesecloth bag with a few spoonfuls of red ocher, and dabbed, or "pounced," the bag over the holes. This caused an outline of little red dots to appear on the plaster. Using the dots as guidelines, the assistants painted outlines of the drawings in red on the wall.

Meanwhile other assistants, led by a chemist, prepared the pigments. They kept a logbook of the pigments' characteristics. Each pigment had its own recipe. For instance, some of the colors lost their intensity if they were ground too fine.

The colors came from natural materials. Some were taken from the earth and could be thousands of years old. Using these pigments ensured that the color wouldn't change during years of exposure to sunlight and artificial light. Pigments came from other sources too. The type of black Rivera used was called Vine Black. It came from France and was made from burned grapevine stems.

The pigments came in chunks, which the artist and his assistants ground on a piece of glass using a marble tool, called an *adze*. Grinding the chunks required a lot of muscle! When an art student named Stephen Dimitroff came to Detroit to volunteer on the project, Rivera put him to work grinding pigments. "I went upstairs and I started grinding colors," the boy recalled. "My arms almost fell off!"

After the pigment was ground to the chemist's specifications, the assistants mixed it with water and daubed it onto a porcelain dinner plate that served as Rivera's palette.

They applied the final coat of plaster to a small section, which Rivera then painted. The section was just large enough for one day's painting. Rivera would have between 6 and 12 hours to paint that section, depending on the temperature and humidity of the room. Because the new plaster covered the red painted outline, Rivera lightly scratched new outlines into it using the handle of a paint-brush. He pinned the original drawing to the scaffold to guide him as he painted.

Kahlo with chemist Andres Sanchez Flores, testing ground pigments

Rivera's assistants had many other tasks. A few days after Dimitroff was assigned to grinding pigments, Rivera asked him to pose as one of the workers in the mural. He asked the boy to take off his jacket to show his shirt. It was winter and the room was very cold. Afterward, Dimitroff became so ill he had to remain in bed for several days. Everyone was so busy that they neglected to bring him food for four days! When Rivera heard about Dimitroff's condition, he was very touched by the boy's dedication.

Once in a while the assistants had a day off from their labor. When Rivera traveled around Detroit to study the various industries, he invited them to come along.

Kahlo was involved with the murals too. From the time they were married, she had helped Rivera with artistic advice. Through the years, Rivera came to rely on her opinion more than anyone else's. When giving advice, she often couched her criticism in a question. For example, if she noticed something in his design that looked out of place, she would gently ask, "Don't you think this is a little . . . ?"

Rivera often became so immersed in his work that he forgot to eat. Kahlo made sure he took breaks for lunch and dinner. To her delight, she found a Mexican grocery store in Detroit, and was able to prepare his favorite meals. She brought a basket full of food and fed not only Rivera, but also anyone else who came to watch him paint.

# *Activity*  **Picture Hunting**

**Diego Rivera was a master at organizing all the images in his murals. See if you can find some of those he included in this one.**

1. A grouchy-looking man wearing a hat and glasses. In his hand he holds a clipboard.

   This is the foreman—the boss watching his workers. Rivera based this subject's facial features on Mead L. Bricker, an important Ford production manager. He was notorious for making the workers move faster by speeding up the assembly line.

2. A group of men and women observing the workers. These unhappy-looking people were painted as a joke by Rivera. They represent the critics who were upset by his mural. One man is a priest. This may have been Father Coughlin, who had a radio show and was a loud voice in favor of the mural's destruction. Interestingly, none of Rivera's critics recognized themselves in the mural.

3. Women sitting at a table. There weren't many women employed at the factory. These women are sewing upholstery for the car seats.

4. A gray-colored man pointing his finger upward. This is Henry Ford teaching a class about his new V-8 engine. His students sit with their hands on their chins. The pose looks like a famous statue by Auguste Rodin called *The Thinker*. In fact, this statue was in the next room at the Detroit museum, and Rivera used it as his model.

5. Two men wearing suits and ties. One is holding a stack of paper. The man holding the papers is William Valentiner. He was the director of the museum who invited Rivera to paint the mural. On the top paper he holds is a dedication that says, "These frescoes, painted . . . while Dr. William Valentiner was director of the Art Institute, are the gift to the City of Detroit of Mr. Edsel B. Ford. . . ." The man next to Valentiner is Edsel B. Ford, the man who funded the project. Rivera included these figures based on a tradition from the Italian Renaissance 500 years earlier. The tradition is called a *donor portrait*. Artists such as Michelangelo often included a portrait of the person who hired them to paint a fresco.

6. A tiny red car. Get out your magnifying glass! In the actual mural, this car is only four inches long. It portrays the very last step in making a car. By painting it so small Rivera is telling us that its production is what is important to him, not the end result.

7. Gray figures crossing a bridge. These are the workers, going home after a long day at the factory. Many of them carry their lunch boxes.

Other Ideas

Play this game with a friend. Describe something you see in the picture and see if your friend can find it. Try this game with other Rivera murals in this book.

Diego Rivera, *Production of Automobile Exterior and Final Assembly*,
detail from *Detroit Industry*, south wall automotive panel, May 1932–March 1933

### The Unveiling

On March 13, 1933, the fresco was finished and the museum officially unveiled it. Visitors to the museum were amazed by what they saw. They had heard the mural's theme was Detroit industry, and many had imagined a traditional, symbolic interpretation. For instance, some expected it would look similar to a painting of the Statue of Liberty. They imagined a picture of a stately woman. In one hand she would hold a lighted torch, and in the other hand, a tiny automobile. Instead, they saw an image filled with real people hard at work. Rivera portrayed working men and women, engineers, and chemists. Even Edsel Ford, the millionaire who donated the funds for the mural, appears—he's hard at work too! Ford is shown at his actual job, designing an automobile.

Some people didn't like Rivera's mural. The factory workers, however, loved it! It showed them as proud, hardworking men and women.

One panel in particular really caused a ruckus. Rivera called it *Vaccination*. In the scene, a nurse comforts a baby as a doctor gives him a vaccination. The animals involved in the vaccination's preparation stand nearby. In the background, three scientists pursue new discoveries. Some people didn't like this scene because they didn't think it was really about medicine. They saw it as a story from the

Bible. "It's baby Jesus in the manger," they claimed. "Surely that's Mary, Joseph, and the three wise men." These viewers found it scandalous to portray this sacred event in such a way. They wanted Rivera's fresco destroyed! For weeks, the controversy raged in the newspapers and radio programs.

In a way, all the controversy helped. Thousands of visitors came to see the mural for themselves. For the most part they were fascinated and pleased by what they saw. After weeks of debate, the controversy died down.

### New York

Rivera's next conquest was in New York City. It was the RCA Building, owned by one of the wealthiest families in America, the Rockefellers. They wanted their new building, located in the heart of Manhattan, to be decorated with the works of several different artists. The overall theme had already been chosen by the building's architects. Each artist was supposed to design a piece based on the description "Man at the crossroads looking with hope and high vision to the choosing of a new and better future."

In March 1933, both Rivera and Kahlo were happy to leave Detroit for New York. Detroit held sad memories of Kahlo's miscarriage. Rivera thought he had done some of his finest work there, but he was excited to begin his next project. They arrived by train at New York's Grand Central Station on a bitterly cold day in March. In less than two days, Rivera was back to work at the RCA Building in Rockefeller Center.

The project began well. Rivera made a sketch of his mural idea and submitted it for approval. A large machine filled the center of the picture. Around it, Rivera included many portraits of people of all classes. There were several little scenes. One portrayed a man grasping the hands of people surrounding him. He seemed to be their leader. Nelson Rockefeller, the project's director, approved the sketch and Rivera set to work.

All was well until someone noticed that the portrait of the man grasping hands resembled Vladimir Lenin. He was a world leader—a *Communist* leader in the Soviet Union. This created a scandal! Newspapers reported that the artist was creating a communist mural with Rockefeller's approval. Lenin's face had not been in the approved sketch. The sketch had been rough, and the features on the portrait weren't detailed.

When Rockefeller asked Rivera to remove the portrait from the mural, Rivera refused. Rivera said that he'd rather destroy his entire mural than compromise his artistic vision. Besides, Rivera reasoned, Rockefeller had known his political

beliefs when he hired him. Almost all of his work expressed his political beliefs, Rivera said, so no one should be surprised.

As newspapers and the public continued to harass him, Rivera continued working on the mural. Kahlo supported Rivera's resoluteness in the matter. Someone gave the order that no photographs could be taken of the work. Guards stood nearby to see that no one disobeyed the order. Secretly, Lucienne Bloch smuggled in a camera under her skirt. She snapped as many pictures as she could without being noticed. (One of these photographs is available on the www.diegorivera.com Web site included in the resources section of this book.) Rivera and his assistants wanted to have photos of their work. Everyone on the project feared the mural would be torn down.

One day in May, while Rivera was up on his scaffold, a group of men suddenly appeared and escorted him from the building. Although the mural was not finished, Rivera was paid in full and ordered to stop work. Workers removed his scaffolds and covered the wall with a large canvas. Later, the mural was destroyed.

Rivera used his original sketches for reference when he reproduced the mural the following year (1934) in Mexico City in the Palace of Fine Arts. It was smaller than the original and there were a

few changes in the details. Also, Rivera changed the title to *Man, Controller of the Universe*. Because this mural has nothing to do with Mexico or Mexicans, many think it is out of place on the walls of the Palace of Fine Arts. It is clearly a work that was created to be exhibited elsewhere.

### Kahlo's View

Kahlo wasn't happy about Rockefeller's decision. But she was delighted that she and Rivera would finally be going home to Mexico. She didn't care for New York. As a visitor, she saw many of its problems.

Kahlo and Rivera lived in New York for nine months. It was 1933, and the Great Depression was at its worst. Many people were out of work. Kahlo saw them standing in soup lines; many were just trying to get enough food to survive. Meanwhile the wealthy still enjoyed champagne and caviar. During an earlier visit to New York, Kahlo wrote a letter to her friend Dr. Eloesser expressing her thoughts:

This upper class is disgusting and I'm furious at all these rich guys here, since I have seen thousands of people in the most terrible misery without anything to eat and with no place to sleep, that is what had most impressed me here, it is terrifying to see the rich having parties day and night while thousands and thousands of people are dying of hunger.

In fact, she could also have seen the problems of the poor near her home in Mexico City. Although Kahlo had participated in rallies to call attention to these problems, she never witnessed them in person. In New York she saw scenes of terrible poverty for the first time.

Kahlo rarely picked up a paintbrush during this time. She did, however, enjoy the company of other artists in New York, including Lucienne Bloch, Stephen Dimitroff, and David Margolis, a sculptor. They liked to play a game called Exquisite Corpse. On a sheet of paper, the first player draws the head and shoulders of a figure at the top of the page. This player then folds the drawing back so that the next person can't see any of the artwork except the end points at the top of the fold. The second player draws the figure's torso, folds it back, and passes it on. The last player adds the lower section of the figure. Then the three players unfold the drawing to reveal the full-figured creature that is a combination of their different artistic visions. The surrealist artists loved to play this game because of the interesting drawings that resulted.

Kahlo also loved going to the movies. One of her favorites was *King Kong*, the story of a huge gorilla who tries to take over New York. She saw the great ape climb the Empire State building many, many times.

For a short time, Kahlo experimented with another art form—frescoes! When she admired a small panel that Bloch was working on, Rivera encouraged her to try it herself. The result was a self-portrait that Kahlo thought was horrible. After writing "Absolutely rotten" and "Oh! boy very ugly" around her image, Kahlo threw it in the trash. Bloch thought it was lovely. She rescued it from the garbage can and took it home. It is now part of a private art collection.

## My Dress Hangs There

Kahlo created only one painting during her stay in New York. She called it *My Dress Hangs There*, and it shows us how homesick she was. In the center of the picture her Tehuana dress hangs on a clothesline, lonely and out of place. In the background, scenes of New York express the bustle and noise of the big city. Kahlo used the painting to poke fun at some of the things she noticed about the United States. On one pedestal, she painted a toilet. This was because U.S. plumbing was very fancy compared to that of Mexico at the time. On another pedestal she painted a golden trophy because competitive sports were so popular. At the bottom she glued on newspaper articles, and pictures of people in soup lines and protest marches. One thing that is not in the picture is Kahlo herself. This is because she didn't feel she belonged in New York.

Frida Kahlo, *My Dress Hangs There*, 1933

# Activity

## My ___ Hangs There

This activity is based on Kahlo's painting *My Dress Hangs There*. In her painting, Kahlo expresses her thoughts and feelings about living in New York. She painted a scene that symbolized the city, and pasted on printed bits and pieces to indicate her feelings. Create a picture that tells a story about something you like or dislike.

### Materials

- Thick sheet of drawing paper
- Coloring or painting materials
- Scissors
- Glue stick
- Photographs or black-and-white photocopies (optional)
- News clippings about yourself or your subject (optional)

1. Choose a subject about which you'd like to express your thoughts and feelings. It can be something that you either like or dislike. Some ideas might include: how you feel about homework; your least favorite food; or something you really enjoy doing, such as playing a musical instrument, dancing, or playing soccer. Think of what you could include in your drawing to tell a story about your topic.

2. Choose one item that represents your subject. For example, if you'd like to draw a picture about playing soccer, your soccer shirt could be the item.

3. Begin your picture by drawing a clothesline, with supports holding it up. In a picture about soccer, the supports could be two trees because soccer is played outdoors. Draw the supports on the left and right side of the paper. Add a clothesline from one support to the other.

4. Draw the item that symbolizes your theme hanging from the line. Make the item large, and place it in the center of the picture.

5. Continue the picture, adding items that relate to your theme. A park scene on a summer day could be the setting for a soccer theme. For laughs, Kahlo painted a toilet in her picture. If you wanted to poke fun at the game of soccer, you might add a smelly sock, a silly looking fan, an excited coach, or other things that relate to the game.

6. Kahlo added printed pieces to her picture. Find newspaper headlines, photos, or text that describes your subject. Magazines may have articles or ads that relate to your subject. Or you might photocopy personal photos. For a soccer theme, the sports section of a newspaper is a good place to look. A photo with you and your teammates would be a great addition. You could also find the letters that make up your team name, cutting them from different magazine headlines.

6. Cut out the items you'd like to include in your drawing. Glue them onto your artwork and incorporate them into the picture.

After being in the United States for three years, Kahlo was ready to go home. But she and Rivera did not return to Mexico right away. Rivera loved living in the United States, and he insisted on staying in Manhattan. He hoped another commission would come his way. As days became weeks, he and Kahlo had terrible arguments. He told her he never wanted to return to Mexico. Even with the latest problems, he felt his work was better respected in the United States than in Mexico.

Rivera could have a terrible temper. During one of their arguments, he grabbed a knife and slashed a painting he had been working on. It was a desert scene of cactus plants, which he had trans-formed into outstretched hands. "I don't want to go back to that!" he screamed.

Finally, Rivera admitted defeat. In December they boarded a ship back to Mexico. Kahlo was overjoyed! She was going home to live—and *work*. She believed she would be inspired by her homeland.

After three years in the United States, Rivera and Kahlo returned to Mexico. Because they were short of funds, friends raised money for their passage home.

This transition would prove difficult for Rivera, who had grown accustomed to the spotlight in the United States. In the coming years, Kahlo would be the artist attracting attention.

Frida Kahlo, *The Frame*, c. 1938

# 6  Kahlo's Fame

Frida Kahlo finally returned home in 1934. She and Diego Rivera moved into a new house designed by their friend, an artist named Juan O'Gorman. Before leaving for the United States, they had decided to have O'Gorman build them this house in San Angel, a suburb of Mexico City. The house consisted of two buildings: a big pink cube, which was Rivera's studio, and a smaller blue cube for Kahlo's studio. Diego's pink house consisted of a large studio with a high ceiling. There he entertained and sold paintings. It had a big kitchen, where they ate most meals. Kahlo's smaller house was more private. It contained a living room/dining room and a small kitchen. The bedroom she and Rivera shared featured a huge picture window. This is also where Kahlo had her studio.

Sitting side by side, the buildings look like giant blocks from a child's toy chest. A bridge from Kahlo's rooftop terrace to Rivera's second-floor studio connected the two buildings. Tall organ cactus plants formed a fence around the house.

Their return to Mexico came at a high price for Kahlo. Rivera finally gave in to Kahlo's wishes to return home, but he wasn't happy, and he blamed all his problems on her. His life just didn't have the sparkle it had in Manhattan, where he'd always been in the spotlight. In Mexico, some people, especially newspaper reporters, criticized his work. Kahlo mentions Rivera's problems in a letter she wrote to a friend in California. In Mexico "the people ... always respond with obscenities and dirty tricks, and that is what makes [Rivera] most desperate since he has only to arrive and they start attacking him in the newspapers." He refused to work, and he decided everything he had done was no good. Eventually he became ill.

Rivera was known to be a *hypochondriac*, someone who imagines he is sick or about to become sick. Not all of his ailments were imaginary. He was hospitalized several times with kidney infections. He had other ailments too, both real and imagined. For all of them, he blamed Kahlo. They had terrible quarrels, and Kahlo would lock Rivera out of her house. Rivera would run back and forth across the bridge, yelling for her to let him in.

A few months after his return to Mexico, Rivera found someone new to shower with affection. This wasn't the first time in four and a half years of marriage to Kahlo that Rivera had become involved with another woman. But this time was different. Rivera's new girlfriend was someone Kahlo loved dearly—her younger sister Cristina. Over the years, Cristina had been a frequent visitor, and she and Frida were very close. Sometimes Cristina modeled for Rivera; he included her image in a mural he painted as early as 1929. One of the first drawings Rivera made upon his return to Mexico was a charcoal portrait of Cristina. Soon afterward the two of them began an affair.

When Frida found out several months later, she was devastated. Later she would say, "I suffered two bad accidents in my life—one

## Talking Pictures

While Kahlo and Rivera lived in the United States, a new art form came to Mexico. In the spring of 1932, the first Mexican talkie (movie with sound) opened. This enabled Mexico's illiterate to learn about their culture at the movies.

A filmmaker named Gabriel Figueroa was a master of this new art form. Born in Mexico City in 1907 (the same year Kahlo was born), Figueroa's first interest was photography. He played the violin, which he studied along with design at Mexico's Conservatorio Nacional. Later he opened his own photography studio. Figueroa excelled as a painter, too. Then he discovered the world of filmmaking.

In 1932, Figueroa got a job working in the Mexican film industry. Three years later he went to Hollywood to learn more about *cinematography*; the art of motion-picture photography. He returned to Mexico after a year and went on to become one of Mexico's (and the world's) most celebrated cinematographers. Figueroa worked with both Mexican and American film companies. In 1948, he made a film version of John Steinbeck's novel *The Pearl*. It's about a poor fisherman whose life is unhappily altered after he finds a valuable pearl. In 1964, Figueroa was nominated for an Academy Award for a movie titled *Night of the Iguana*. Both movies were beautifully filmed in Mexico, which is where Figueroa did most of his work.

Before talkies, the mural movement was the best means of teaching history to people who couldn't read. Talking pictures changed everything. On a single Saturday, the movies drew more people than the number who would see Rivera's murals in an entire year.

The fact that talkies challenged the importance of mural painting didn't stop Rivera from creating art. From 1934 to 1940, he didn't create any new frescoes. Instead, he went back to his easel. During this time, he painted some of his finest canvases, such as 1935's *The Flower Carrier* (see page 38).

was the streetcar collision, and the other was Diego." Greatly distressed, Kahlo cut her beautiful long hair and stopped wearing colorful Mexican costumes. These were two things about her that Rivera had always adored.

During the next year she painted only two pictures. One of them, *A Few Small Nips*, is based on a news story Kahlo had read. It is a picture of a woman lying dead, after being stabbed by her husband. Her blood fills not only the bedroom scene, but also the picture's frame. Kahlo covered the plain wooden frame in smears of red paint. Once again, she channeled her feelings through her art. It was too painful to portray her own problems directly, so she created an image of another tragedy. She told a friend that she painted this picture because she herself had come close to being "murdered by life." Forty-five years earlier, an artist Kahlo and Rivera both admired had portrayed a similar scene. In 1890, José Guadalupe Posada had created a small engraving titled *A Victim of Francisco Guerrero, "El Chalequero."*

Kahlo tried living apart from Rivera. But even when they lived apart, they saw each other constantly. After several months of living on her own, Kahlo decided to return to her blue cube in San Angel. In a letter to Rivera, she wrote "... all the rages I have gone through have served only to make me understand in the end that I love you more than my own skin." Rivera was glad she came back and was sorry he had hurt her.

Once again, the couple began to throw parties for their friends. They entertained visiting artists and celebrities. They even hosted two very famous political figures, Leon Trotsky and his wife, Natalia.

Kahlo forgave her husband and sister. But her life was changed. She decided she should try to be less dependent on Rivera. One way to achieve this, she thought, was by supporting herself financially. She knew that was possible through her art. Up until that time, she had painted whenever she felt like it. Sometimes she was productive, but often she stopped painting for months at a time. She created wonderful pictures but usually gave them away as gifts. Now Kahlo was determined to support herself through the sale of her paintings. Rivera agreed with her decision. He knew she was happiest when she was painting.

Kahlo focused diligently on her art. She spent more time painting, became more disciplined, and worked hard to improve her technical skills. In one year she produced more paintings than she had in all her married years. They were wonderful pieces. But Kahlo wasn't confident about her work.

She was not a shy person, but she seemed shy about her art. She wasn't good at promoting her

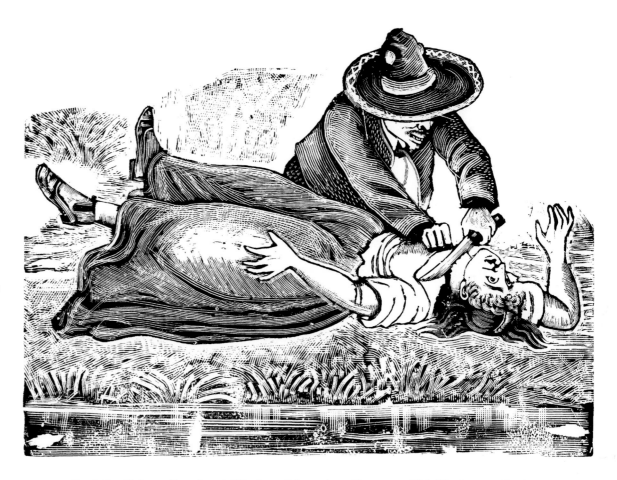

José Guadalupe Posada, *A Victim of Francisco Guerrero, "El Chalequero,"* 1890

# Leon Trotsky

In 1937, two world-famous guests came to live at Kahlo's family home, the Casa Azul. They were Leon Trotsky and his wife, Natalia. The Trotskys had been thrown out of their own country, Russia. Like the Russian leader, Joseph Stalin, Trotsky was a Communist. But Stalin and Trotsky differed on how to run the country, and Stalin did not like to be questioned. Trotsky had been the right-hand man of the former Communist leader, Vladimir Ilyich Lenin. When Lenin became ill in 1922, Stalin took power. He and Trotsky became bitter enemies, and in 1929, Stalin ordered Trotsky to leave the country. For nine years, Trotsky and his wife lived in central Asia, Turkey, France, and Norway.

Leaving Russia didn't stop Trotsky from voicing his ideas. He continued to write articles that people read all over the world. To put an end to this, Stalin sent assassins to find Trotsky and kill him. Russia put pressure on countries that had welcomed the Trotskys as guests in the past. In 1936, the Trotskys didn't have any place to go. Rivera admired Trotsky and persuaded the Mexican government to allow him to enter the country. President Lazaro Cárenas agreed to grant them political *asylum* (safety). When they landed in Mexico in January 1937, Kahlo was there to meet them. She took them to her family home, the Casa Azul.

Rivera and Kahlo knew it was dangerous to associate with the Trotskys. But it was also exciting! Once Stalin found out where the Trotskys were hiding, there was no telling what would happen. Rivera had great fun playing secret agent. After relocating Kahlo's father to the home of one of her sisters, Rivera turned the Casa Azul into an impenetrable fort and hired guards to watch over his guests.

After two years, the Trotskys moved to another hideout, only six blocks from the Casa Azul. The reason for the move isn't clear. Some think that it was because Rivera had become jealous of all the attention Kahlo showered on Trotsky, and asked him to leave. Trotsky and Kahlo did spend time together. She affectionately called him "the old man" (he was 28 years older than Kahlo) and Little Goatee. She even gave Trotsky a self-portrait, painted especially for him. He enjoyed Kahlo's attention but constantly criticized her for smoking cigarettes. Some people think that they passed little notes to each other in the books he lent her.

There was tight security around the Trotskys' new quarters, and guard towers commanded a view of the street. Early one morning, 20 men dressed as police tricked the guard into opening the gate. They rushed in with their machine guns, and fired into the Trotskys' bedroom. Miraculously, Trotsky and his wife saved themselves by jumping under their bed.

Three months later, however, Trotsky's luck ran out. One of Stalin's agents succeeded in killing him as he sat reading at his desk. Rivera and Kahlo got more than their share of excitement when the police named them as suspects! Rivera had been a suspect in the first attempt on Trotsky's life. However, after this second (and successful) attempt, Kahlo and her sister Cristina were brought in for questioning as well. They were suspects because they had once had dinner with the assassin, Ramón Mercader. The women were questioned by police for hours and held in jail. After two days of questioning it was apparent that neither of them was involved. The sisters were finally allowed to go home. During this time, Rivera was in San Francisco painting the Unity mural. When he learned that Kahlo was being held by the police he was very upset. (See page 88 to learn about Rivera's great escape to the United States.)

paintings. She fretted over the prices she asked. Later, when people began to buy her pieces, she often would say she felt sorry for the purchaser. "For that price they could buy something better," she often said.

Rivera couldn't have agreed less! Even during their separation, Rivera was Kahlo's greatest promoter. He thought her paintings were fabulous, and he told everyone who would listen. He knew it was important for the public to see her work and urged Kahlo to exhibit her paintings.

## Kahlo's Success

It wasn't long before Kahlo found success. In 1938, at age 31, she entered four paintings in an exhibit for the first time. It was at a small gallery near the University of Mexico. As usual, Kahlo downplayed the gallery, her paintings, and how they were received. In a letter to her friend Lucienne Bloch, she wrote (in English):

I have painted about twelve paintings, all small and unimportant, with the same personal subjects that only appeal to myself and nobody else. I send [*sic*] four of them to a gallery, which is a small and rotten place, but the only one which admits any kind of stuff . . . four or five people tell me they are swell, the rest think they are too crazy.

Kahlo, 1932

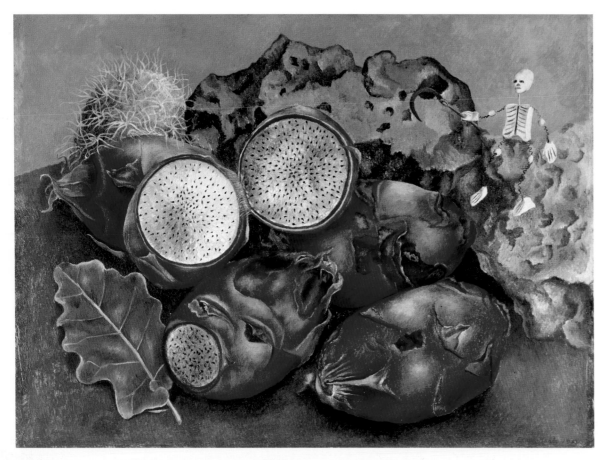

Frida Kahlo, *Still Life: Pitahayas*, 1938

Surely this wasn't the case. But even if it was, Kahlo was a hit. One of the people who thought her art was "swell" was an important New York art dealer named Julien Levy.

Meanwhile, Rivera actively promoted Kahlo's work. One summer day, Edward G. Robinson paid a visit at their home in San Angel. Everyone knew of the American actor, who usually played tough-guy roles in gangster movies. But not too many of his fans knew he was an avid art collector. On this visit, he had come to buy some of Rivera's artwork.

Rivera had other ideas. After presenting his own work, he pulled out several of Kahlo's paintings, which she had hidden away. Robinson was so impressed that he immediately bought four paintings for $200 each. When Kahlo found out, she was thrilled! Her self-confidence was boosted even further when Julien Levy offered her a solo exhibit in New York.

## A One-Woman Show in New York

That autumn Kahlo left for New York alone. The opening night of her exhibit was a grand event. Among the crowd were world-famous artists such as Georgia O'Keeffe. Wealthy patrons and connoisseurs were on hand too. Kahlo looked fabulous. In her bright Mexican costume, she was a perfect complement to her paintings.

78

Kahlo's exhibit, which included 25 paintings, did quite well. No one in the crowd had seen a group of paintings quite like these. The press was delighted with her, although some articles described her as "Little Frida" and "Diego Rivera's German-Mexican wife." By the show's end, Kahlo had sold about half of her paintings. This was remarkable in 1938 with the effects of the Great Depression still apparent.

Kahlo enjoyed this time in New York much more than earlier visits. Now *she* was in the spotlight. Her three-month stay included numerous parties hosted by her patrons. She even befriended Nelson Rockefeller; she was no longer furious with him for destroying Rivera's mural.

This was Kahlo's entrance into New York's art scene and Rivera had coached her about what to do. For example, he helped her make a list of important people to invite to the opening. He advised her on how to attract art patrons, meet dealers, and get publicity. If she was successful, she'd return to Mexico with many commissions.

One prospective patron was Clare Boothe Luce, the editor of *Vanity Fair* magazine. In a letter to Kahlo, Rivera wrote, "You ought to do a portrait of Mrs. Luce even if she doesn't order it from you. Ask her to pose for you and you will get a chance to speak with her." He also suggested that Kahlo read the plays Luce had written. That way she might get ideas on how to portray her subject. Kahlo never did the portrait, but Luce did commission her to paint the portrait of a friend.

Another wealthy art collector named Conger Goodyear fell in love with a painting Kahlo had already sold to someone else. It was a self-portrait of Kahlo with her pet monkey, Fulang-Chang. Goodyear commissioned Kahlo to paint a similar picture. She painted it in her hotel room, finishing it in a week.

New York seemed much more exciting now. Kahlo enjoyed taking time to explore the city, visiting places like Chinatown, Little Italy, and Broadway. She went window shopping, looking for interesting, inexpensive trinkets. Everywhere she went, she caused a sensation. Kahlo was not shy about standing out in a crowd. Julien Levy remembered a day he and Kahlo were walking down a street, followed by a flock of children. When the two entered a bank, all the kids followed. As the doorman tried to round them up, the excited children kept calling, "Where's the Circus?" They thought Kahlo, in her colorful costume, was part of an act.

She also caught up on the latest American movies. She loved movies by the Marx Brothers and Charlie Chaplin. Beyond the entertainment, sitting at a movie enabled Kahlo to rest. It was hard for her to walk long distances because her right foot

## A Sparkling Smile

Kahlo never smiles in her self-portraits or photos. That's not because she was always sad. In fact, Kahlo loved to laugh and be silly. She also loved to eat sweets! Because of this, some of her teeth were decayed.

Her problems were solved when she had her teeth capped. The caps were removable and memorable. For special occasions, she wore gold caps that were decorated with diamonds. Her friend, Parker Lesley, remembered one such occasion. That particular evening Kahlo and Rivera arrived late to a performance at the Palace of Fine Arts, in Mexico City. All eyes were on Kahlo!

No one paid any attention to the dance performance. . . . Everyone stared at Frida, who wore her Tehuana dress and all Diego's gold jewelry, and clanked like a knight in armor. She had two gold incisors [teeth] and when she was all gussied up she would take off the plain gold caps and put on gold caps with rose diamonds in front, so that her smile really sparkled.

When the performance stopped for intermission, Kahlo walked through the crowded lobby. The crowd parted for her as if she were a queen.

# Georgia O'Keeffe

One of the guests at Kahlo's opening was the famous artist Georgia O'Keeffe. Born in Sun Prairie, Wisconsin, in 1887, O'Keeffe was the second of seven children. As a child, she received art lessons at home. When she was 12, her mother arranged for her to take drawing and painting classes from an art teacher. Each Saturday she traveled seven miles in a buggy pulled by a horse to her art class. By age 17, she had decided to become an artist, and she began studies at the Art Institute of Chicago. Later, she moved to New York to study, and then on to Texas and South Carolina to teach art. After learning the techniques of other well-known artists, she worked to develop her own unique style.

Proud but secretive, O'Keeffe sent a few pieces of her art to a friend from college named Anita Pollitzer who lived in New York. The paintings arrived with strict instructions not to show them to anyone. But her friend was so excited when she saw the work that she disobeyed O'Keeffe's orders. She brought them to Alfred Stieglitz, a famous photographer who owned a gallery. Thrilled, he hung them in an exhibit. When O'Keeffe found out she was furious! Eventually, though, she not only forgave Stieglitz, but she married him as well.

O'Keeffe first met Kahlo and Rivera during Rivera's exhibit at the Museum of Modern Art in 1931. By then she was very well known. Her specialty was flowers, which she painted in a style unlike that of anyone else. While most artists would portray a vase full of flowers, O'Keeffe tended to paint only one or two huge blooms. They were much larger than life—sometimes 40 inches tall! You can look right into her flowers, as if you are a bumblebee.

Even though they were from different countries, Kahlo and O'Keeffe had several things in common. Both artists portrayed their love of nature in their work. For example, Kahlo painted juicy slices of watermelon and tropical fruits (see page 78). The colorful fruit is cut open, exposing its seeds. Like O'Keeffe, Kahlo makes sure we see the brilliant colors and interesting shapes of nature.

The two artists had similar marriages, too. Each married an older man who was already an established artist, their husbands diligently promoted their work, and neither woman had children.

Kahlo and O'Keeffe were good friends, but they didn't see each other often. They spent time together during Kahlo's stay in New York in 1938. Years later, when O'Keeffe was traveling through Mexico, she visited Kahlo at the Casa Azul.

Their greatest similarity is their fame. Today, Georgia O'Keeffe is considered the most important female artist from the United States in the early 20th century. Kahlo is held in similar esteem in Mexico.

was giving her problems again. Even so, she enjoyed her visit thoroughly.

She also enjoyed the company of photographer Nickolas Muray. Muray was very talented; his photographs appeared regularly in fashion magazines such as *Harper's Bazaar* and *Vanity Fair*. He was also handsome and kind. A fan of Kahlo and her work, he had bought one of the paintings in her exhibit. He also spent time photographing her. A romance was beginning to bloom. Kahlo felt she was falling in love.

After a very successful visit, Kahlo left New York for France.

## A Paris Hit

In January 1939, Kahlo set out for Paris. Twenty years after Rivera's success with cubism there, Kahlo exhibited a very different style. The exhibit, organized by the poet André Breton, was called *Mexique*. During his visit to Mexico, Breton was dazzled by the new things he saw. He wanted the people of Paris to see them too—especially his surrealist discovery, Frida Kahlo.

When she arrived Kahlo realized that the exhibit was not what she expected. She was unhappy about how Breton had designed the exhibit. In addition to her 17 paintings, he included souvenirs, such as sugar skulls and religious *retablo* paintings.

## André Breton

Breton was the self-proclaimed founder of the surrealist movement, which started in Europe and included writers, poets, photographers, and painters. Salvador Dalí, for example, was one of the most famous surrealist artists.

Breton first saw Kahlo's work while in Mexico on a lecture tour. Without hesitation, he declared her part of his group. Kahlo thought Breton was a pompous bore and usually tried to avoid him when he came to visit Rivera. Even though she ignored him, Breton was captivated by Kahlo and her art. To him, her small paintings were incredibly powerful. He said her art was like "a ribbon around a bomb."

Kahlo did not consider herself a surrealist. In surrealism, the art appears dreamlike. Kahlo's paintings were based on her real life, not her dreams. "I never knew I was a surrealist," she said, "till André Breton came to Mexico and told me I was." As she later pointed out, "I never painted dreams, I painted my own reality."

For example, someone might think the skeletons in Kahlo's paintings are something out of an odd dream. But for Kahlo, skeletons were part of her culture, not a surrealist creation. The toy skeleton in her painting *Pitahayas* is something she could have collected. For meals, she liked to decorate the table with flowers, fruits, toys, and even a chipmunk in a cage. She often included a toy or one of her pets in her paintings of fruit. This was simply a reflection of her personality.

Nickolas Muray with Kahlo in her studio, 1941

# Activity  Story Framing

Sometimes Kahlo used personal touches to create a colorful border around her images of herself. The colors and images she used add to the story she is telling about herself. In her 1938 painting *The Frame* she surrounded herself with flowers and birds. Make a portrait of someone and frame it with things that the person enjoys.

## Materials

1 sheet of 10-by-12-inch drawing paper

Pencil

Ruler

Painting supplies (such as tempera) or coloring supplies (such as crayons or markers)

1. Using a pencil, draw a rectangle 2 inches from the edge of the drawing paper. This area is for your art's frame.

2. Draw a portrait inside the rectangle. Fill the area with your chosen figure, from the top of his or her head to just below the shoulders.

3. Design a frame that contains objects that represent the interests of your subject. If the portrait is of your little brother, for example, you might include his favorite treats, such as ice cream and candy, as well as a few of his favorite toys, such as a kite, toy car, or balloon. Kahlo filled her frame with colorful flowers and parrots. Fill the frame area all the way around the picture. Don't limit the images to appear only in the frame area. Let each image flow, some from the painting onto the frame, and some cut off by the portrait image.

4. Once your sketch is complete you are ready to add color. If there are areas in the frame that do not contain an object, fill these with a different color than that of the portrait's background. This creates a border around the portrait and helps that border stand out as a work of art itself.

These were things Breton had picked up while visiting Mexico. In Kahlo's opinion, these folk pieces didn't belong in her exhibit.

Breton was not a very organized person, which caused the exhibit to be delayed. When it finally opened, a lively crowd filled the gallery. Well-known artists who lived in Paris, such as Pablo Picasso, Joan Miró, and Wassily Kandinsky came to the opening and praised her work. The show was not a financial success. Kahlo herself, however, was a smash!

The French considered Kahlo a work of art. She made quite an impression walking down the streets of Paris in her Tehuana costumes and pre-Columbian jewelry. Elsa Schiaparelli, the Parisian clothing designer, created a gown she called "Madame Rivera." Kahlo's hand, covered with rings, was featured on the cover of French *Vogue*. Although she received one favorable review, the show was not a critical success. Breton's wife, Jacqueline, thought the French were too nationalistic to be interested in the work of an unknown foreigner. The French seemed far more interested in Kahlo the spectacle than Kahlo the artist.

Rivera's old friend Pablo Picasso admired Kahlo and her work. To show his admiration, he gave her a pair of unusual earrings. Each is shaped in the form of a dangling hand. In appreciation, she painted a self-portrait in which she wore the earrings.

The surrealist artists in Paris welcomed her into their circle. She met painters, poets, and writers who took her to their favorite café hangouts and jazz clubs. She enjoyed playing games, such as Exquisite Corpse, with the surrealists. However, she quickly grew bored listening to their theories. In her opinion, they would have been better off doing more painting and less talking.

Kahlo stayed in Paris until her exhibit closed in March. By the show's end, only one painting had sold, but it sold to a very special customer. One of the most famous museums in the world, the Louvre (LOO-vr), purchased a painting titled *The Frame*. It is a small self-portrait surrounded by the bright colors of Mexico, complete with two parrots. Kahlo would be the first Mexican artist in the Louvre's collection—quite an honor! Not even the master, Diego Rivera, could make this claim.

## Art Detective: How to Spot a Surrealist Painting

Here are some characteristics that help distinguish a surrealist painting:

- Dreamlike! The picture appears to be something like you'd see in a strange dream.

- Real but unreal! You recognize what the picture is of, but odd items are combined. An apple so large it takes up an entire room. A little girl entwined in the stem of a huge sunflower.

- Keep looking! There's so much happening—the more you look, the more you find. Maybe you'll even find something as wild as a desert scene decorated with clock faces that look like melting cheese.

Frida Kahlo, *Self-Portrait*, 1940

# 7  An Unhappy Homecoming

Frida Kahlo returned to Mexico in 1939 as a star following her success in both America and France. But her glow soon faded. Once back home, she learned that Rivera wanted a divorce. Maybe he was involved with someone else, or perhaps he had learned about Kahlo's romance with Muray. Whatever the reason, his desire to leave hurt Kahlo deeply. She admitted that she and Rivera had a stormy relationship. Still, she didn't want their marriage to end. When reporters called to get her side of the story, she had little to say. Kahlo granted Rivera a divorce without argument. Once again she expressed her grief in her paintings.

Shortly thereafter, Kahlo painted a self-portrait that was very different from her previous ones. It was neither pretty nor charming. In *Self-Portrait* (1940), instead of posing in the beautiful jewelry Rivera had given her, she wears a thorny vine around her neck. It grips her so tightly that drops of blood drip from the thorns. Behind her shoulder, a black cat looks ready to pounce. Even her pet monkey, Caimito de Guayabal, holds the thorns in a way that could pull them tighter, hurting Kahlo more. A dead hummingbird hangs from her necklace. The shape of its wings matches the arch of Kahlo's eyebrows. There are myths about hummingbirds, and Kahlo is telling us something by adding one to this painting. In Aztec mythology, the spirits of dead warriors returned to Earth

as hummingbirds. To the Aztecs, the hummingbird symbolized a return to life. At the top of Kahlo's picture, delicate flowers sprout wings and fly away. Aztecs also believed a dead person's spirit might return as a beautiful butterfly. In Mexican folklore, dead hummingbirds were used as charms to bring luck in love. Perhaps Kahlo included the hummingbird and butterflies to symbolize her hope for happier times.

## On Her Own

After the divorce, Kahlo moved back to the home where she had grown up, the Casa Azul. Once again, she had problems with her health. She complained of shooting pains in her back, and her doctors disagreed about what was wrong. Some recommended spinal surgery. Since the trolley accident, she had had several operations to correct problems with her right leg and back. "I'm not sick. I am broken," she once said. She didn't look forward to another operation.

Her newest doctor, Juan Farill, didn't think Kahlo needed an operation. Instead, he believed that her spine needed to be stretched. He suggested bed rest, along with a strange type of traction. A photograph of Kahlo shows her undergoing this treatment. Her chin is propped in a sling while an apparatus pulls the sling

# *Activity*    **Kahlo-Style Self-Portrait**

Kahlo's self-portraits have several things in common. She looks directly out, filling the space from the top of her head to just below her shoulders. The background often contains flowers, leaves, or stormy skies. Kahlo used symbols to tell us what she was thinking about or how she was feeling. Using ideas from the self-portraits by Kahlo on pages 72, 84, and 132—*The Frame* (1938), *Self-Portrait* (1940), and *Self-Portrait as a Tehuana (Diego in My Thoughts)* (1943)—create a portrait of yourself. Whether you are happy or sad, include symbols and colors that express your state of mind.

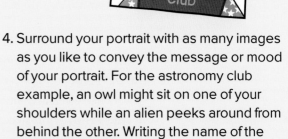

### Materials

Mirror

Drawing paper

Pencil

Painting or coloring supplies of your choice

1. This self-portrait is like a chapter from a book about you. It will tell a story with images instead of words. Decide what type of story you'd like to tell. It can be about how you are feeling at the moment, something you have been thinking about, or a story about something that happened to you. For example, you might want to express what you think about a club you are in, such as the astronomy club.

2. On a separate page, draw little symbols or images that relate to the story you want to tell. Think of as many images as you can and then draw them. You don't have to use them all—you are the artist so you get to decide. For example, symbols for the astronomy club might include planets, rockets, stars, an owl (representing the night sky), and a telescope. Use your imagination. For example, you might include a UFO or an alien creature.

3. Now you are ready to begin drawing your picture. Start by drawing a self-portrait in pencil. Use a mirror for reference. To follow Kahlo's style, include the top of your head to the middle of your chest. Your eyes should be looking straight ahead, and the expression on your face should show how you feel.

4. Surround your portrait with as many images as you like to convey the message or mood of your portrait. For the astronomy club example, an owl might sit on one of your shoulders while an alien peeks around from behind the other. Writing the name of the club on your shirt will give viewers a clue about your story.

5. Kahlo often filled the area behind her portraits will lush plants or stormy skies. Fill up the background of your picture with things that fit your subject. For the astronomy club theme, a starry night sky complete with a planet and rocket might fill the background.

6. Be sure that the expression on your face indicates how you are feeling about what is happening in the picture.

7. Add color to the picture until you have completely covered the page.

8. Don't forget to sign your name somewhere on the picture. Include the date, too, as Kahlo usually did.

Here are some other thematic ideas for your portrait.

• If you want to show that you are feeling loved, you might include an item that relates to someone who loves you. Perhaps the background is filled with the flowers that grow in your grandmother's garden. Or you might show a pattern from the plate she uses to serve you cookies. You might include your lovable pet cat, bird, or mouse snuggled against your neck.

• If you want to show that you're not crazy about homework, you might create a background in the form of a blackboard filled with equations. Perhaps a pile of books balances on top of your head. An owl, which represents staying up late, sits on your shoulder. Be sure that the expression on your face conveys your reaction to all this homework.

upward. Every day, for several hours, she was hooked up to a 40-pound weight that was attached to the strange contraption. Kahlo was unable to move while the weight pulled her head, neck, and spine up toward the ceiling. It was torture.

## Reunited

By the summer of 1940, Kahlo had given up hope that Farill's treatment would help her. Kahlo and Rivera had been divorced for six months. Rivera was back in San Francisco painting a mural at the Golden Gate International Exposition. This time, the public was invited to watch Rivera while he worked. Thousands of visitors filed past his scaffold as part of an *Art in Action* exhibit. Other artists, such as sculptors, joined Rivera as part of the show. The theme of Rivera's mural was *Pan American Unity*.

While Rivera was in San Francisco, he and Kahlo exchanged letters. Rivera learned that Trotsky had been assassinated. When he heard that Kahlo had been held for questioning in the murder, Rivera became very upset. Even though they were divorced, he still cared deeply for Kahlo. He was also concerned about her deteriorating health, and he feared that stress would make things worse. For advice, Rivera decided to turn to their old friend,

Dr. Eloesser. Eloesser had been Kahlo's physician during their earlier visit to San Francisco. He and Kahlo had kept in touch through letters ever since. Eloesser knew her problems well.

Eloesser had always believed that many of Kahlo's problems were caused by stress. Her ailments seemed to get worse after her divorce. He thought the best thing for her would be to remarry Rivera. Eloesser knew Rivera would be in San Francisco for several months working on the mural. So he devised a plan. Eloesser would persuade Kahlo to come to him for medical advice. Without Rivera or Kahlo knowing it, Eloesser would also play Cupid!

The first part of his plan worked. Back in Mexico, Kahlo's doctors were suggesting surgery. Eloesser persuaded Kahlo to fly to San Francisco for a second opinion. When she arrived, he put her in the hospital for a month of tests, and found no need for spinal surgery. But Eloesser discovered Kahlo had grown dependent on brandy and tequila. "I used to drink to drown my sorrows," she once said. "Now they have learned to swim." He recommended bed rest and no alcohol.

Next, Eloesser had to talk to Rivera. He told Rivera that Kahlo's problems weren't caused by disease. Her suffering was brought on by nerves because of the divorce. He told Rivera that there

## Rivera's Great Escape

It was fortunate that Rivera was invited to participate in San Francisco's International Exposition in 1940. It was a good time for him to leave Mexico. After the first attempt on Trotsky's life on May 24, 1940, the police considered Rivera a suspect. They planned to bring him in for interrogation, but Rivera outwitted them.

He had help from a beautiful movie star from the United States named Paulette Goddard. She was in Mexico to have Rivera paint her portrait, and she stayed at a hotel across the street from his studio. One evening, she happened to look out her hotel window and noticed strange goings-on outside Rivera's house.

As Goddard watched, she became terribly excited. She telephoned Rivera's studio. "Diego," she said with a trembling voice, "if I know anything about gangster movies, brother, you're on the spot. The cops are swarming around your studio. And they look like they mean business."

Rivera didn't know what the police wanted, but he assumed it meant trouble. Quickly, he devised a plan to escape. An artist named Irene Bohus happened to be visiting him, so he asked her to help. She walked out of his studio carrying as many canvases as she could under her arms. Slowly, she moved toward her car, bidding Rivera long, loud good-byes. Meanwhile, he ran back to his studio and turned on all the lights. It seemed as if he was back at work. Quickly, he sneaked around and hid in the backseat of Bohus's car. All the while Bohus pretended to be calling up to him in his studio. She piled the canvases on top of Rivera, concealing him completely. Jumping into the car, she whisked him away. He hid out (possibly in his lawyer's home) until he was able to obtain the necessary papers to enter the United States. With the help of the U.S. Embassy and the U.S. Consulate, Rivera was able to fly to Brownsville, Texas (with Paulette Goddard). After being questioned briefly by immigration officials, he was able to secure a one-year visa.

Later Rivera learned that witnesses had claimed they saw his car in the neighborhood the night of Trotsky's attempted murder. Of course, Rivera had nothing to do with the crime. But another famous artist did. David Alfaro Siqueiros, who was also a fresco painter, was guilty of trying to assassinate Trotsky. He was a member of Los Tres Grandes, a group that included Rivera and José Clemente Orozco. Siqueiros was a loyal follower of Stalin. When he learned that Stalin wanted Trotsky murdered, he decided to lead an attack. The police did succeed in arresting Siqueiros.

Even though Rivera was out of the country, he didn't feel completely safe. While painting his mural for *Art in Action* in San Francisco, he hired an armed guard to stand beside his scaffold. He feared Trotsky's followers might think he had been in on the plot and send someone to kill him.

was only one way for her to recover—they must remarry. Rivera admitted their separation was having a bad effect on him too. Rivera had to ask Kahlo several times before she accepted. Finally, on December 8, 1940, Rivera's birthday, they remarried. And Dr. Eloesser's predication came true. Over the next few months Kahlo's health did improve.

Kahlo and Rivera's second marriage took place in a San Francisco courtroom, opened on Sunday just for the occasion. Only two of their friends were on hand for the quick ceremony. That same day, Rivera went back to work painting his mural. There, in front of the crowd that had gathered to watch the *Art in Action* exhibition, Rivera took off his white dress shirt. Everyone must have laughed when they saw his undershirt covered with the imprints of Kahlo's bright pink lipstick.

## The Casa Azul

Two weeks after they remarried, Kahlo returned to Mexico in time to spend Christmas with her family. Rivera remained in San Francisco to finish his mural. In February, he packed his bags and went home to Kahlo at the Casa Azul. (He kept his studio at the San Angel home.)

With her mother gone and her father no longer living there, Kahlo enjoyed redecorating the home in which her life had begun. She filled the Casa Azul with brightly colored folk art she'd found during her travels through Mexico. There were earthenware pots from Oaxaca (wa-HOCK-a); copper kettles from Santa Clara; and glasses, cups, and pitchers from Guadalajara (gwad-a-la-HAR-a), Puebla, and Rivera's hometown, Guanajuato. The decor was truly Mexican.

The inner rooms glowed with deep blues, brilliant yellows, and vibrant orange-reds. The high white ceilings and wood beams were set off by yellow cane furniture and terra-cotta pots.

The kitchen was the center of their home. Kahlo decorated it with blue, yellow, and white tiles. Her favorite clay pots sat on the counters. On one wall, Kahlo hung tiny clay cups. They spelled out "Frida" and "Diego."

Outside, the courtyard was a lush jungle of flowering plants. It was perfect for Kahlo's menagerie. She loved animals! Songbirds and parakeets warbled and chattered in their cages. She had a collection of cats, dogs, monkeys, turkeys, an eagle named Gertrude Caca Blanca (Gertrude White Poop), and a deer.

Two of Kahlo's favorite pets were monkeys. One was Fulang-Chang, which means "any old monkey." The other was Caimito de Guayabal, which means "guava-patch fruit." Both were Mexican spider monkeys.

Eight years earlier (1932), Rivera and Kahlo share a tender moment as he works on the *Detroit Industry* mural.

One visitor remembered meeting Fulang-Chang. "I came for lunch, and a spider monkey promptly sat on my head and took the banana out of my hand. I had to balance the monkey, whose tail was around my neck, as I showed my sketches." Sometimes, however, these monkeys were not so friendly. One had a crush on Rivera and didn't like rivals. When a famous movie star came to visit, the jealous monkey tried to bite her. Rivera loved the attention—he thought the quarrel between the monkey and the beauty queen was hilarious.

Bonito, Kahlo's pet parrot, was often present at meals, too. Walking across the table, he nibbled morsels from everyone's plate. Everyone loved Bonito's beaky kisses. Another parrot often startled new guests by shrieking, *No me pasa la cruda!* ("I can't get over this hangover!").

Frida Kahlo, *Still Life with Parrot*, 1951

One guest, Ella Wolfe, a cofounder of the American Communist Party, recalled a visit at Kahlo and Rivera's home. "Nobody had a stranger household than the Riveras," she said. "There were monkeys jumping through the window at lunchtime. They just jumped up on the table, took some food and left. And there were seven hairless Xolotl (show-lotl) dogs named after leaders of the Communist Party. That was fun because they answered to their names."

Even when their pets misbehaved, which was often, Rivera and Kahlo showered them with love. Once one of the dogs urinated on a watercolor Rivera had just finished. Rivera grabbed a knife and chased the dog around the house. But when he cornered it, he picked the dog up and said, "Lord Xolotl, you are the best art critic I know."

## Building a Dream

The demand for Kahlo's work increased after her New York and Paris exhibits. She was invited to participate in shows with other well-known artists, too. Shortly after her return from Paris, she painted two pictures for the International Exhibition of Surrealism in Mexico City. The year was 1940 and Kahlo was 32 years old. The exhibit had already been to Paris and London. Its arrival in Mexico City was the biggest cultural event of the year. It was an honor for Kahlo to have her work join this exhibit.

Kahlo's work also remained popular in the United States. She participated in several group exhibits at MOMA and other museums. Along with these shows came sales. For example, Sigmund Firestone, a wealthy American engineer, commissioned a pair of self-portraits by Kahlo and Rivera. "Please make them both on the same size canvas as I intend to always keep them together in memory of our pleasant acquaintanceship," he wrote.

Rivera was busy creating portraits of wealthy patrons. Famous artists have made money this way for centuries. Rivera was still the most famous painter in Mexico; everyone wanted to own a Rivera.

Rivera was planning other creative endeavors as well. Since his return from Europe in 1921, he had collected 60,000 pieces of art from Mexico's ancient civilizations. These ancient people, including the Mayans and Aztecs, were incredible artisans. Rivera studied their cultures, collected their work, and praised them in many of his murals. Now he had the dream of constructing a great building to honor their cultures and accomplishments. He wanted this building to have a design unlike any modern building in Mexico. In fact, it would look like an ancient temple. It would be the perfect home for his collection. Together, Rivera and Kahlo worked to build this museum. They called it Anahuacalli (ah-nah-wah-CA-yi).

# *Activity* Fruit with a Friend

**Kahlo's still-life paintings often include an unexpected guest. She liked to add one of her pets or a favorite toy sitting among the juicy pieces of fruit. Make a still life that adds your own special touch.**

## Materials

Tabletop

Fruit

Toy or household pet

Drawing paper

Pencil

Painting or coloring supplies, such as tempera paint or crayons or markers

1. Arrange fruit in a pleasing display on the tabletop itself, in a bowl, or on a plate. Kahlo often cut open pieces of fruit or included slices. Watermelon and kiwi fruit make colorful models when sliced open.

2. Add something fun to your display. Include a doll or stuffed animal perhaps. If you use a toy, position it among the fruit. Or you might include a pet hamster or goldfish. If you include a pet that's not in a cage, you may not be able to get it to stick around and pose. Decide where you'd like to place the image in the picture. Make a quick sketch of the pet and use it for reference.

3. Draw the still life in pencil, including the sketch of your pet, if necessary.

4. Once the drawing is complete, retrace the sketch with paint or crayons or markers and add bold, bright color to your drawing.

Diego Rivera, detail from panel 1, *Pan American Unity* mural, 1940

# 8 The Art of Mexico's Past

Diego Rivera was fascinated by the art of ancient Mexico. Ever since his return from Europe in 1921, he had collected pre-Columbian art (from the Aztec, Mayan, and other ancient Mexican civilizations). This type of art was easy to find. People were discovering artifacts throughout Mexico. One site, Tlatilco (tlah-TIL-co), had been discovered inside a brickworks in Mexico City. Rivera traveled there whenever he could to see what treasures had been unearthed. Sometimes he and Kahlo used the pieces from his collection as models in their own artwork.

People knew that Rivera spent every cent he could scrape together on pre-Columbian art. Sometimes he spent his money on an ancient object, such as a little stone figure, instead of on food. This was a problem when he was a young man married to Guadalupe Marín. Once she got so angry that she ground up one of his figurines and served it to him for dinner. She decided that if he was going to spend the household budget on pieces of stone, he should have to eat them, too. But her rage didn't stop Rivera's spending sprees.

Kahlo knew about Rivera's spending habits too. "Frida used to scold me sometimes for not keeping enough money to buy such prosaic [ordinary] things as underwear," Rivera said. Bit by bit, his collection grew. By 1942 he had 60,000 pieces, and he needed somewhere to put them. Kahlo found just the right spot.

On the edge of Mexico City, near Coyoacán (Kahlo's birthplace), lies a lava bed called the Pedregal. Kahlo had once purchased a parcel of this land to help house a refugee of the Spanish War and his family. Later, when Rivera decided to build, he bought additional land surrounding it. *Pedregal* (peh-dre-GAHL) means "rocky area." Nothing grew there except cactus and thorn bush.

Rivera envisioned another use for the land. He thought it was the perfect site to build a museum for his pre-Columbian collection. It would be his museum and art studio. When the time came, Rivera thought, it would also be his tomb. The only fitting design, he decided, would be a Mexican-style pyramid. He called the building Anahuacalli. In *Nahuatl* (NAH-wa-tel), the language of the Aztecs, this means "house of the valley of Mexico."

Rivera designed the building himself. He described it as a combination of traditional Aztec, Mayan, and Rivera styles. Rivera liked the natural landscape of the area, especially the cactus that sprang up from crevices in the lava. Rivera wanted to build the museum in harmony with the terrain, so he chose construction materials to match. He made the walls from basalt, a dark stone common in the area. When seen from a distance, the building seems to loom up out of the lava.

Inside, a maze of narrow passageways leads to different rooms. Like the exterior, the inner walls are made of cold, gray stone.

## Uniting Mexico and America

In *Pan American Unity*, Rivera hoped to illustrate the great contributions of all the cultures of the North American continent—from the ancient Mexicans to the modern-day Americans. At the time he was painting the mural, Rivera said that he was hoping to create "a real American art . . . the blending of the art of the Indian, the Mexican, the Eskimo with the kind of urge that makes the machines [industrial America]."

In the mural Rivera depicts many scenes. In a Hollywood scene, he shows Charlie Chaplin making a movie. In a scene filled with inventors, Henry Ford is holding a part for an automobile. In a construction scene, an architect is studying a blueprint. Meanwhile, Helen Crlenkovich, the 1939 national diving champion, is shown tumbling across the mural performing one of her famous dives. It's a bright, colorful work filled with action.

There aren't many windows. Rivera placed his favorite idols throughout the maze, in small niches. Shafts of sunlight from narrow windows above illuminate the exhibits. The feeling on the interior is dark and mysterious—just like an Aztec temple. The ceilings were decorated with brightly colored mosaics Rivera created himself. They were inspired by the abstract designs of pre-Columbian art.

Today the building has three levels. Rivera's spacious art studio occupies one of them. Huge windows stretch from floor to ceiling, letting light pour into the workspace. A rooftop terrace looks out over the lava bed. In the distance, two snow-capped mountain peaks rise from the landscape. The view is fabulous!

The artifacts are displayed in many areas of the museum. Rivera placed some of his best pieces on the lowest level, throughout the narrow passageways.

Rivera worked on Anahuacalli until the end of his life. The cost of such an extravagant building was enormous. As Rivera made money selling his artwork, he continued building. Construction was finally complete seven years after Rivera's death.

The life and art of ancient Mexico was a passion that Rivera pursued for most of his life. He studied the Aztec, Mayan, Olmec, and Toltec cultures—the hopes, fears, and ideas of these people who lived as long ago as 1300 B.C.

## Honoring Ancient Mexico in Murals

In 1942, Rivera began creating a series of frescoes at the National Palace. There were 11 panels, and they all depicted ancient Mexican civilizations. He had already finished a series at the National Palace titled *Mexico of Tomorrow*. In that series, Rivera had illustrated his ideas about Mexico's future. Now, along the open corridors of the first floor, he began a beautiful tribute titled *Mexico of Yesterday*. In this series, Rivera included scenes of native peoples from long ago. He shows them as he imagined they had once lived: planting grain, building temples, and dancing to honor the corn god. In other panels Rivera included the skillful artisans he admired. He depicted them at work—weaving, sculpting, and creating tremendous works of art. It took Rivera nine years to complete this series.

Two years before starting *Mexico of Yesterday* in Mexico City, Rivera created similar scenes at the *Art in Action* exhibit in San Francisco, the mural he was working on in 1940 when he and Kahlo remarried. He titled his San Francisco mural *Marriage of the Artistic Expression of the North and South on This Continent*. It's also known as the *Pan American Unity* mural.

## Rivera's Inspirations

Of the five panels that make up *Pan American Unity*, one is dedicated to Rivera's favorite topic: the artisans of ancient Mexico. In it he shows "the creative genius of the South." Through his illustrations, Rivera was able to share his knowledge about Mexico's past. He knew that many people who came to see the mural in San Francisco would not be familiar with the ancient cultures south of the U.S. border. By painting this panel, Rivera was able to introduce viewers to these cultures. From the skillful Olmec craftsmen to the poet-king of Texcoco, Rivera painted the story of Mexico's past. He believed the story was very important. He thought all Americans should be inspired by the creative spirit and artistic accomplishments that had occurred on their own continent long ago.

Look carefully at Rivera's fresco panel on page 92 to see how he tells the story of ancient Mexico.

## The Rubber People

More than 3,000 years ago, the Olmec (Ole-mek) people carved statues from volcanic rock. These works include giant heads standing nine feet high! Some experts think these are portraits of the rulers of that time.

"El Castillo" pyramid at Chichén Itzá

Olmec Head

# Lord Xolotl: A Dog and an Inspiration

In his *Pan American Unity* mural, Rivera painted his dog, Lord Xolotl, obediently sitting at the feet of an Olmec artisan. Rivera and Kahlo were crazy about this breed of little dogs called Xoloitzcuintli (show-low-its-queen-tlee). Once bred by the Aztecs, the dogs have no fur. This oddity gives them their alternate name, Mexican Hairless. Even without fur, their little bodies are nice and warm. The ancient Aztecs used them as bed warmers and hot-water bottles for their aches and pains. Another use for the dogs, however, was as a food source.

For Rivera and Kahlo, the little dogs were a great deal of fun. The two artists included Xoloitzcuintlis in several paintings. Kahlo holds one in a self-portrait. In the same picture you can see a pre-Columbian figure and a monkey peeking out from behind her shoulder.

*Xoloitzcuintli* means "dog of Xolotl." Xolotl was the Aztec god of lightning. The Aztecs believed that Xolotl pushed the sun toward the ocean at sunset and guarded her during the night on her dangerous journey through the underworld. Xolotl, the Aztecs believed, also greeted people when they died, and accompanied them on their journey in the afterlife. He helped them cross a mystical river and overcome many obstacles on their way to the spirit world, Mictlan.

People who lived in ancient Colima made chubby little ceramic dogs. Many of these red pot-bellied dogs have been found in tombs there. Often they were placed looking anxiously at their masters. Some people think the dogs of Colima might represent Lord Xolotl. Perhaps they were put in tombs to accompany a loved one to Mictlan.

Look carefully at the image of Henry Ford teaching about engines, and you'll see Rivera's imagination at work. The engine has pointy ears, four little legs, and a tail. It's a dog!

Colima Dog

Diego Rivera, detail from *Detroit Industry*, south wall predella panel, May 1932–March 1933

The Olmecs also carved designs on large blocks of stone, some of them 17 feet tall. Each block is a monument called a *stela* (stee-la). A common stela decoration was a jaguar holding a human in its jaws. Jaguars prowled many places in Mexico, and some pre-Columbian cultures considered them magical. In *Pan American Unity*, Rivera shows three Olmec artisans carving a stela. One artist has a jaguar tattoo. You can see its tail and spots.

It wasn't easy to make the giant sculptures. First the rock had to be brought down from the mountains. Olmec workers hauled the rock up to 60 miles to a village. The Olmecs devised a way to float the rocks down rivers on top of rafts. Some rocks weighed more than 40 tons. That's about as heavy as 25 cars!

Once the rock was in place it was sculpted. But the Olmecs didn't have metal tools. One way they formed shapes was by rubbing damp sand over the rock to wear it away. It was like using sandpaper to carve the stone. Just imagine this long, difficult process!

Olmec artisans also crafted ceramics and intricate clay figures. Because the statues and pottery are made of hard rock and clay, they've survived for thousands of years. But many aspects of the Olmec culture and civilization are lost to history. For instance, we don't know what they called them-

# Activity  Olmec Head Carving

**Carve your own version of an Olmec head. Make it in the Olmec style, or invent something new. Hundreds of years from now, archeologists might dig it up and study it!**

## Materials

2 cups used, dry coffee grounds

1 ½ cups cornmeal

¼ cup salt

Mixing bowl

Warm water

Plate

Toothpick

1. Combine the coffee grounds, cornmeal, and salt in a bowl.

2. Slowly add warm water, a few spoonfuls at a time. Mix the ingredients with your hands. Add just enough water to make the mixture stick together.

3. Form the mixture into a ball and pack it tightly, as if you are making a snowball. You're creating a miniature boulder.

4. Set the ball on a plate to dry. Depending on your area's climate, it will take at least one day to dry. It will dry faster in a warmer and less humid climate. In humid or cooler areas, the process will take longer.

5. Turn your miniature boulder into a carved portrait. To do this, think of the shape as if it were someone's head. Use a toothpick to carve a face. The material will be pretty crumbly and easy to carve.

# Activity

## Aztec Tattoo

**Many pre-Columbian cultures painted decorations on their bodies. They applied natural pigments to a clay or stone stamp, and pressed it onto their skin. Some stamps were flat; others were in the shape of small wheels. The wheels were rolled over the skin and made long border-like designs.**

### Materials

- Small potato
- Potato peeler
- Knife (ask an adult to help)
- Toothpick
- Tempera paint, any color
- Small plate

1. Peel the potato.

2. Cut the potato into three ¼-inch slices to create three circular disks.

3. Carve a design around the edge of each disk. To do this, cut wedges or curves along its ¼-inch side. For example, make two cuts each to form several *V* shapes around the edge. Repeat for each slice.

4. Stack the disks and pierce with a toothpick, pushing it through the slices until they are centered on the pick.

5. Let the slices dry overnight.

6. Once your stamp is prepared, you are ready to apply a tattoo. To begin, pour a small amount of paint onto a plate.

7. Holding the stamp by each end of the toothpick, roll the stamp in the paint. Be sure to cover all the edges around the slices.

8. Apply the tattoo to your own arm or leg, or decorate a friend's arm. Hold each end of the toothpick and slowly roll the stamp over the skin.

---

selves. The name *Olmec* comes from the Nahuatl language, and means "rubber people."

Archeologists think that the Olmecs tapped rubber trees for the sticky liquid that makes rubber. It's likely that they coated items such as baskets with rubber to waterproof them. The Olmecs also made the first soccer ball (although the rules were different). Long after the Olmec civilization disappeared, people from another culture gave them their name.

## The Power of the Jaguar

One animal Kahlo didn't have as a pet was a jaguar. At one time these creatures roamed the Mexican countryside. People found them both amazing and terrifying. The ancient Olmecs, Aztecs, and Mayans thought these large cats were so powerful they must be gods. The people tried to harness the power of the great cats. Special Aztec warriors, called jaguar knights, dressed as jaguars when they went into battle. They believed this would give them the jaguar's strength. Others imitated the cats by tattooing jaguar images on their bodies.

Many pre-Columbian peoples decorated their bodies with art. They'd paint designs on themselves for festivals and rituals. Sometimes they used a stamp dipped in paint and pressed it onto their skin. Ancient people also used stamps to decorate pottery. Rivera had many stamps in his collection.

Stamp design
showing a jaguar
and serpent motif

## Little People of the Earth

Rivera's collection included many simple clay figurines, probably made by peasants. Archeologists usually discovered these at burial sites. Experts think the ancient people made the figurines to keep the dead company in the afterlife. Other figurines were used for rituals. They helped a priest ensure a successful harvest or birth. After their magic worked, people broke the figurines and threw them away. At first you might think that all these figurines look the same. But examine them more closely and you'll see that each has its own personality. Some are chubby, some are happy, and some look surprised. Rivera delighted in his collection of little clay people.

Rivera also had in his collection many fancy jade and gold pieces, fit for ancient kings. In his *Pan American Unity* mural, Rivera painted artisans hard at work making jewelry from gold. The ancients greatly respected the skills of these craftsmen.

Male and Female Figures,
100 B.C. to A.D. 400

**99**

# Activity

## Pre-Columbian Companion

**Make your own little buddy in a pre-Columbian style. She might like to sit on your computer monitor or desktop to keep you company while you do your schoolwork.**

### Materials

Newspaper

Self-hardening clay, such as Mexican pottery clay (available at a local craft store)

Container of water

Toothpick

String (optional)

Magnet (optional)

1. Cover your work area with newspaper.

2. Roll an egg-sized piece of clay between your hands to warm it up.

3. Divide the clay and form the shapes to make a small figure. Make a torso, two arms, a head, and two legs.

4. Attach the pieces. To do this, apply a bit of water where the pieces join together. Using a toothpick, scratch the areas to be joined, mixing clay from each side to affix firmly. The water will help further blend the clay and make the connection stronger.

5. Add details to the face. Use a toothpick to sculpt features. Or form features out of the extra clay. For example, to make eyes, press a toothpick into a small ball of clay to make an indention such as that found on a coffee bean.

6. Add a whimsical hairdo, earrings, or any accessories you like.

7. Let the figure dry.

8. Set your creation in a place where it can keep you company.

As an alternative, you might make only the head. Pass a toothpick through it above the ears, and from side to side, to make a channel. You can use it as a bead and, after it's dry, string it on a necklace. Or glue a magnet on the back and put it on your refrigerator.

Female figure from Tlatico, 1500 to 900 B.C.

## The Pretty Ladies

In 1942, workers in Mexico City made a discovery that couldn't have pleased Rivera more. They were digging up clay to make into bricks. As they dug they found bones and pottery. Right there in Rivera's own city, workers discovered a site that was full of artifacts from long ago. It was called Tlatilco, which means "the place where things are hidden" in Nahuatl.

There was a series of female figurines that are now called "pretty ladies." The ladies, numbering in the hundreds, have a few things in common. They have unusually short flipper-type arms, very chubby thighs, and narrow waists. But they all have different whimsical hairdos. Many of the pretty ladies were found in tombs, but some turned up in open fields. Archeologists think these artifacts were planted in the four corners of each farmer's cornfield to ensure good harvests.

## Gods and Goddesses

Not all little clay people look whimsical; in fact, some seem very serious. These are considered idols. They served an important role in pre-Columbian religions. Ancient people worshiped and feared the gods or spirits the idols represented. They believed that the gods controlled everything and had to be respected. The sun wouldn't rise and

Two examples of chacmool

the rain wouldn't fall unless the gods were happy. To please them, people made offerings to these statues. They gave the statues flowers, shoots of corn, and sometimes even live sacrifices. People danced, sang, and played music to make the gods happy.

## Yaqui Deer Dancers

The Yaqui people of northern Mexico were one tribe that danced for their gods. They performed their sacred deer dance to create harmony with the deer spirits. Because the Yaqui people lived on deer meat, they worshiped the gods who provided the deer. The Yaquis believed their dance would increase the deer population and enhance their hunters' skills. In his *Pan American Unity* mural, Rivera shows the Yaqui deer dancers playing musical instruments and dancing.

# *Activity* **Tin-Art Greeting Card**

Pre-Columbian artists used wonderful designs to decorate their pottery and murals. This design represents the god of dance, a monkey named Ozomatli (oh-so-MAH-tli). It was also the symbol for the 11th day of the month. Make an Ozomatli greeting card in a colorful tin-art style that is popular in Mexico today.

Flat stamp depicting Ozomatli, God of Dance

## Materials

- Aluminum foil
- Scissors
- Photocopy of ancient design pattern such as the jaguar and serpent motif from page 99 or the monkey from this page
- Toothpick
- Permanent markers, several colors
- Construction paper
- Glue stick

1. Fold a 12-by-6-inch piece of aluminum foil in half so that it is 6-by-6 inches.

2. Place the foil on a soft surface, such as a magazine.

3. Place the pattern of a pre-Columbian design on top of the foil.

4. Trace the pattern by pressing a toothpick along its lines. This will make an indentation in the foil.

5. Lift the pattern to see the indented design in the foil. Color the lines with a marker.

6. Fold a 12-by-9-inch piece of construction paper in half to make a 6-by-9-inch card.

7. Trim the foil around your design.

8. Glue the colored foil onto the front of the card.

One method the Aztecs used to please their gods was human sacrifice. They battled neighboring tribes to capture enemy warriors. Then they sacrificed their prisoners in elaborate ceremonies.

One of the figures Aztec artisans often carved was a *chacmool* (chac-mole). Today, chacmools may seem welcoming when we meet them at a museum or an Aztec pyramid. Propped on their elbows, with heads turned to one side and knees bent, it seems as if they are just waking up from a nap. The bowls that rest on their stomachs suggests they fell asleep after a snack. These statues didn't seem so welcoming to the Aztecs' prisoners. Part of the sacrificial ritual required that the victim's heart be cut out and offered to the gods. The captors placed each victim's heart in the chacmool's bowl.

## King Netzahualcóyotl

One king thought there were other ways to please the gods. He had the tongue-twisting name of Netzahualcóyotl (neh-tzah-wahl-COY-ohtuhl). Born in 1403, he was the king of the Texcocans (tex-COH-cans). They lived next to Lake Texcoco (tex-COH-coh) in central Mexico, near the Aztecs. Luckily, Netzahualcóyotl had a pact with his warrior neighbors and didn't have to fear invasion.

Netzahualcóyotl is known as the poet-king. He thought the gods would be pleased if people created

Diego Rivera, *Netzahualcóyotl, Poet and King of Texcoco*, detail from panel 1, *Pan American Unity* mural, 1940

beautiful things for them, such as artwork, songs, and poems. He was also an inventor. One legend credits him with developing a flying machine—500 years before the Wright brothers! Rivera gives tribute to Netzahualcóyotl in his mural by painting him and his invention.

Both men and women wore jewelry. If you look closely, you'll see that Netzahualcóyotl is wearing ear spools. These were large disks, often made of jade, that, like pierced earrings, attached through holes in the earlobes. He's also wearing a necklace with a skull-shaped ornament. Kahlo loved to wear pre-Columbian pieces like this one.

## Modern-Day Models

Rivera studied the art and myths of ancient Mexico. He read everything he could, and visited remote sites. He often used ancient stone figures as models for his murals. They popped up in some very unusual places.

Coatlicue (ko-aht-LEE-kway), the stern-looking Aztec goddess of earth and war, sometimes appears

**Diego Rivera, detail from *Production of Automobile Exterior and Final Assembly*, *Detroit Industry*, south wall automotive panel, May 1932–March 1933**

in Rivera's frescoes. The Aztecs believed she was the mother of Huitzilopochtli (we-tsee-low-POCH-tlee), the powerful god of war. Coatlicue was a very important goddess who required human sacrifices. One sculpture that inspired Rivera depicts Coatlicue as an aging warrior woman. She's dressed in a warrior's skirt of netted rattlesnakes. She has been decapitated. Two streams of blood in the form of coral snakes are spouting from her neck. Together, they form what looks like a monster's head. She wears a necklace made of hands and hearts, with a skull hanging down.

If you look closely at one of the machines in Rivera's *Detroit Industry* mural, you'll see it looks very much like Coatlicue. The machine is a stamping press, which fabricates auto parts from sheet metal. Rivera thought the stamping press and the goddess had something in common. They both needed a type of human sacrifice. The machine required men to give their hard labor.

## Look to the Past

To Rivera, the art of ancient Mexico was the most wonderful in the world. Most North Americans were likely to style their homes and clothing according to what was happening across the ocean in Europe. Women wore the latest Paris fashions and decorated their homes with copies of furniture in styles made popular by kings and queens. These styles had names like Queen Anne and Louis XIV. If a home featured a statue of a dog, it would most likely be an English hunting dog, not a pot-bellied Colima.

Rivera thought North Americans should look to their own past for design inspiration. He often gave lectures to share his artistic ideas and information about the ancient history of the Americas.

## Anahuacalli

Late in his life, Rivera gave Anahuacalli to the people of Mexico. He always intended to donate his museum to the citizens of Mexico and chose to do it during his lifetime. He didn't live to see the completed building, which opened as a museum in 1964. Experts consider Rivera's 60,000-piece collection one of the finest of its kind. Upon entering Anahuacalli, visitors see a message from Rivera. Inscribed on a stone are his words: "I return to the people the artistic heritage I was able to redeem from their ancestors."

Many aspects of Mexico inspired Rivera and Kahlo. They both worked hard to build a temple honoring their pre-Columbian ancestors. Rivera looked to these past cultures for many of his artistic ideas. But Kahlo also found great inspiration in the creations of modern-day Mexican folk artists.

Coatlicue, Aztec, Tenochtitlan, ca. 1487–1521, stone h. 3.5 m. Mexico City. Museo Nacional de Antropologia

Clay pot from the state
of Michoacán, Mexico

# 9 Folk Art and Fiestas

Frida Kahlo loved the art of modern-day Mexico as much as Diego Rivera loved pre-Columbian art. She was especially struck by the work of local artists. These self-taught artisans often created folk art, such as pottery, for daily use. Other works were strictly for decoration. Kahlo collected them all. One of her favorite destinations was the market, where street vendors sold their art.

Over the years she had become friends with the market vendors, and they looked forward to her visits. "She was full of joy and love of life," one friend said. "She had invented her own language, her own way of speaking Spanish, full of vitality and accompanied by gestures, mimicry, laughter, and jokes." Eagerly, the vendors would bring Kahlo up to date on their lives and family dramas. Kahlo couldn't have been happier—she loved to gossip.

The market was full of delicious scents and dazzling colors. There were fruit stalls stacked high with yellow papayas, green limes, and red chilies. Kahlo used these colorful fruits in her still-life paintings. She captured one of her favorite pets inspecting a luscious arrangement in *Still Life with Parrot* (see page 90). She included beautiful flower displays in her paintings too. In the market, flower vendors sold colorful blossoms fresh from their gardens. Later, when students came to her home for art lessons, Kahlo found another use for the fruits and flowers she bought at the market. She made a game of seeing which student's arrangement made the most interesting still life.

The market was also a fiesta of wonderful scents. Everywhere the smell of fresh-baked bread and roasted chilies lingered in the air. Kahlo usually left the market with some sort of treasure. It might be a doll or a basket she just couldn't live without. Sometimes Kahlo included one of these treasures in a painting. In her still life *Pitahayas* (see page 78), one of her toy skeletons sits on a piece of lava. She was excited by brightly colored pottery, too. And she loved decorations! During holidays, she bought elaborate trinkets for her fiestas. With her cook, Eulalia, she chose the ingredients for the incredible dishes they'd concoct for lucky dinner guests.

## A Cause for Celebration

Kahlo used any excuse to have a party. Fortunately for her, the Mexican calendar is filled with holidays and celebrations. Many require their own special decorations and foods. One of Kahlo's favorites was the Day of the Dead. In the springtime, she enjoyed Holy Saturday, the day before Easter. Mexicans celebrate this day by setting off firecrackers that are attached to large papier-mâché creations called Judas figures.

# Activity

## Papel Picado Pizzazz

Any festive occasion calls for colorful Mexican banners called *papel picado* (pah-PELL pee-CAH-thoh). You can create these decorations by snipping pieces from tissue paper. Use special colors or designs for the occasion you're celebrating. Celebrate Mexican Independence Day with green, white, and red banners. Or cut out shapes, such as flowers and butterflies, for a summer party.

### Materials

- Colored tissue paper
- Scissors
- String
- Glue stick

1. Cut a 12-by-12-inch square of tissue paper.

2. Fold the tissue in half so that it is a rectangle measuring 6 by 12 inches.

 3. Starting at one of the 6-inch ends, make fan folds about 1 ½ inches wide.

4. Cut small shapes along the edges of the folded tissue. For example, cut in the shape of the letter *V*, or make the shape of one side of a heart or star. Cut the entire shape from the tissue so that it releases from the folded tissue. You will not use the pieces that are cut out.

5. Unfold the rectangle to see your designs. A *V* shape cut will look like a diamond.

6. Fold one edge of the tissue down 1 inch. This is how you'll hang the decorations across the string (see below for further instructions on this). Set aside while you make more banners.

7. Repeat steps 1 through 6 to make enough banners to cover the area you want to decorate. A 12-foot space will take 11 or 12 banners.

8. Tie a long piece of string above the party area.

9. One by one, apply glue to the 1-inch flap, hang the cut tissue over the line, and press the edges together to secure.

Clay pot in the form of a chicken, from the state of Michoacán, Mexico

Kahlo loved all the holidays that celebrated Mexico, especially September 16, Mexico's Independence Day. In September, the markets are full of the colors of the Mexican flag—green, white, and red—from decorations such as flags and *papel picado* ("tissue-paper banners"). Similar to the U.S. holiday Fourth of July, this day celebrates Mexico's 1821 independence from Spain.

Kahlo always began preparing for festivals days in advance. She was very patriotic and liked to show pride in her country. She bought little Mexican flags and stuck them all around her house and garden. At meals, the flag decorated her centerpieces of stacked fruit. Flags showed up in her paintings and in the planters that lined the house's hallways. She also bought little caps, shaped like the ones Mexican soldiers had worn in 1821. She handed these caps out to neighborhood children, along with wooden swords and cardboard bugles.

On Independence Day, Kahlo welcomed friends into her home for a fiesta. She set the table with her beautiful pottery and hung red, green, and white banners. With help from Eulalia, Kahlo prepared traditional holiday treats. One of the most

## Butterfly Spirits

In the autumn, Mexico's landscape bursts with blooming flowers. Millions of monarch butterflies fly in from the north, adding to the natural beauty. During the summer, these orange-and-black butterflies live as far away as Canada. But around the time of the Day of the Dead in early November, they return to Mexico's fir forests in Michoacán (meech-oh-ah-KAHN). The trees dazzle as hundreds of monarchs cluster together on branches. They seem to be everywhere, fluttering in the sunshine. No wonder the ancient people of Mexico thought they were magical.

Throughout the centuries, people believed the monarchs were the returning spirits of their ancestors. Beautiful butterfly patterns decorate pre-Columbian art. Kahlo used them in her paintings too.

# *Activity* Kahlo's National Flag Rice

Make this delicious dish on Mexico's Independence Day, September 16 or any day you feel like having a Mexican fiesta. The three colors of rice combine to look like the Mexican flag. It's not just delicious, it's a work of art!

## Ingredients

2 green onions

½ cup fresh cilantro leaves

3 cups cooked white rice

Juice of 1 lime

⅓ cup salsa

2 tablespoons tomato paste

## Materials

Cutting board

Knife for chopping (with help from an adult)

Measuring cup

2 mixing bowls

Mixing spoon

Large rectangular plate

Yield: 6 ½-cup servings

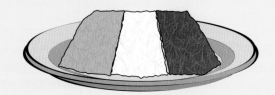

1. Finely chop the green onions and cilantro. Stir them into a bowl containing 1 cup of rice. Add lime juice. This will make up the green part of the flag.

2. In a separate bowl, mix the salsa and tomato paste. Stir in 1 cup of white rice. This will be the red part of the flag.

3. Arrange the rice on a plate in vertical stripes in this order: green, white, and red.

While enjoying the delicious rice, remember that on the Mexican flag the green field stands for hope and symbolizes the independence movement. The white field stands for the purity of the Catholic faith. The red field stands for union and symbolizes the unity of the Spaniards who joined forces to help Mexico gain independence from Spain, and it symbolizes the blood of the national heroes who died in pursuit of this cause. In the middle of the field of white is an eagle perched on a prickly pear cactus devouring a snake. It symbolizes an Aztec heritage legend.

colorful dishes was National Flag Rice. She'd color the rice white, red, and green, and arrange it to look like the Mexican flag. The red rice was colored with salsa and the green with cilantro.

In the springtime, the day before Easter Sunday is a lively time in Mexico. It's called *Sabado de Gloria* ("Holy Saturday"). On this day, the people tie large papier-mâché figures with firecrackers and hang them from tall buildings and posts. Known as Judas figures, they represent one of Jesus Christ's disciples. According to the Bible, Judas was responsible for Jesus' arrest because he pointed him out to the Roman soldiers. Throughout Mexico, artists make the colorful figures and sell them in the market. They often look like devils or skeletons, and they're larger than life—sometimes 10 to 12 feet tall! Some Judas figures look like real people, such as unpopular politicians.

On Holy Saturday, people set fire to the Judas figures, which burn or explode. Sparks fly with sizzling pops as Judas is punished, year after year, for his sin.

Sometimes, Kahlo liked particular Judas figures too much to blow them up. She thought they were fun. To her they were like good-natured larger-than-life dolls. She decorated the Casa Azul with them, inside and out. Sometimes, she even dressed them in her own outfits. She kept one of her favorites on top of her canopied bed. This Judas

figure and others appear in some of her paintings. Rivera referred to Kahlo's canopy Judas figure as her boyfriend.

## Day of the Dead

Many of Kahlo's paintings feature skeletons or other symbols of death. Even her portrait of Luther Burbank (see page 50) shows a skeleton entwined in roots and resting peacefully. It's not surprising that every November Kahlo faithfully celebrated a holiday that used skeletons as its main symbol.

In ancient times, Mexicans believed that the dead returned to earth once a year. Later, with the adoption of the Catholic religion, ancient traditions combined with the church's celebration of All Souls' Day. On November 2, Mexican families and friends join together to remember those who have died. It's a happy occasion.

Families plan for this welcome days in advance. All through the towns, bakeries sell special bread called *pan de muerto* ("bread of the dead"), which is molded in the shape of bones. Skulls made of sugar come in many sizes, with bright tinsel eyes. Throughout Mexico, there are picnics at the cemetery. People also create special shrines, called *ofredas*, in their homes. They are beautifully arranged, usually on a table covered with an especially nice cloth. Often marigolds, the traditional

Sugar skulls

# Activity  **Day of the Dead** *Ofrenda*

Admirers of Kahlo and Rivera still make memorials to them on the Day of the Dead. Celebrate November 2 by making a little ofrenda to honor someone *you* miss, or someone you admire, such as a famous artist or a relative who died before you were born. The purpose is to remember the wonderful things the person did, and to celebrate his or her life. Maybe you'd like to honor someone you admire from history, such as Abraham Lincoln, Marie Curie, or Martin Luther King Jr. On November 2, display your ofrenda in a special place.

## Materials

Photograph of the person you wish to honor

Construction paper

Scissors

Glue stick

1 2-by-2-foot piece of cloth

Tabletop for display

Items that represent the person's individuality, such as a type of hat he or she wore or a favorite book or musical instrument

Favorite foods or treats your chosen person enjoyed

Shoebox with lid

Flowers

1. Fold the construction paper in half to create the shape of a greeting card.

2. Glue a portrait of your subject on the cover of the card. When setting up your *ofrenda*, you'll stand the card up, on edge, to display it. For example, if you are honoring Abraham Lincoln, use a photocopy of a drawing or photograph of him.

3. Gather other images or objects that relate to your subject. Perhaps the person is known for something he or she said. If so,

write the quote on another small piece of paper and mount it on the construction paper as you did with the portrait. For Lincoln, you might write down a sentence from the Gettysburg Address. Perhaps you have pictures of something your subject did, or something that suggests where he or she lived. A photo of a log cabin would be a fitting image for Lincoln.

4. What other symbols might suggest your subject? Perhaps he or she wore a certain costume. Find a picture or make a replica of an object that relates to your subject. For Lincoln, you might make a small top hat out of black construction paper.

5. Think of what type of food your subject enjoyed or, if you didn't know the person, imagine what foods might have been his or her favorites. Prepare a favorite dish. Or fill a plate with fruit, candy, or other treats.

6. On November 2, display your memorial. Begin by setting up the base of the ofrenda. Set a lidded shoe box on a table or wherever you'd like to display your memorial.

7. Drape the shoe box with a cloth that covers part of the tabletop, too. The cloth should cover at least an 18-by-18-inch section of the table. The box will create a raised platform under the cloth.

8. Arrange your selected items on the covered platform in a pleasing way. Place the photo on top of the box. Surround it with the other items you gathered. Add flowers, too. Marigolds are the traditional flower for ofrendas. Perhaps your subject liked other flowers as well.

flower of the dead, adorn the table along with the deceased's favorite foods. Many Mexicans believe that the dead partake of the food in spirit. Afterward, though, the living family members enjoy the tasty offerings.

Like many other Mexicans, each year Kahlo created an ofrenda dedicated to the memory of deceased family members. When preparing a celebration, Kahlo enjoyed the help of younger family members. Her sister Cristina's children often lent a hand. She also spent time with Rivera's daughters from his marriage to Guadalupe Marín. Marín's daughter, Guadalupe, remembered one of the times she helped with the preparations. One year, she went with Kahlo to gather decorations for an ofrenda. They visited Carmen Sevilla, an artist who made papier-mâché skeletons and sugar skulls. The skulls remain a tradition on the Day of the Dead. Names of both the living and the deceased often appear on a skull—written in icing. Kahlo bought large skulls with the names of her mother and father. Others had "Diego" and "Frida" written on them. Her smallest skulls had the names of the children in the family. All these—plus dancing skeletons, flowers, candles, photographs, and favorite foods—she placed on a table honoring her parents. The Casa Azul was transformed into a place of honor, respect, and celebration for the dead.

Papier-mâché bride and groom skeletons

# Activity

## Pan de Muerto ("Bread of the Dead")

Celebrate the Day of the Dead with a special treat called *pan de muerto*. Mexicans make this bread in round loaves topped with strips of dough that resemble bones. It takes a while to make this bread because it requires time to rise. But it's easy and fun, and the bread tastes great! You'll need an adult helper.

### Ingredients

3 cups all-purpose flour, divided

1 ¼ teaspoons active dry yeast

½ teaspoon salt

2 teaspoons anise seeds

¼ cup white sugar

¼ cup butter or margarine

¼ cup milk

¼ cup water

2 eggs, beaten

### Glaze

1 egg white, beaten

1 tablespoon sugar

### Materials

Stovetop and oven

Measuring cups and spoons

Large mixing bowl

Small pot

Small mixing bowl

Mixing spoon

Electric beater

Plastic wrap

Baking sheet (lightly greased)

Pastry brush

To make the bread dough:

1. In a large bowl, combine 1 cup of the flour and the yeast, salt, anise seed, and sugar. Set aside.

2. In a saucepan, heat the butter, milk, and water until very warm but not boiling.

3. Pour the warm liquid into the flour mixture and beat until combined. Add the eggs, and beat in another cup of flour. Slowly add the remaining cup of the flour.

4. Place the dough onto a lightly floured surface and knead 10 minutes until smooth and elastic. To knead, press the heels of your hands into the dough, fold the dough over, and press again. Continue to knead using the weight of your upper body to put pressure on the dough. Kneading is necessary to develop the gluten in the dough, which helps the dough to rise properly.

5. Place the dough into a lightly greased bowl and cover with plastic wrap. Set it in a warm place for about 1 ½ hours. The dough will double in size.

6. Leave the dough in the bowl and punch it with your fist. Pull off a handful of dough and shape the rest into a round loaf. Shape the remaining handful of dough into "bones" and place on top of the loaf. Place the loaf onto a lightly greased baking sheet, loosely cover with plastic wrap, and let rise in a warm place for about an hour.

7. Take the beaten egg white and brush it onto the surface of the dough. This is the glaze.

8. Sprinkle sugar on top of the loaf.

9. Bake in a preheated 350°F oven for 40 minutes. Let cool for 1 hour. This bread is sweet and delicious to eat plain. Enjoy!

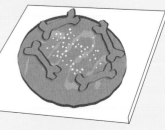

## A Folk-Art Influence

Kahlo's own work was influenced by the Mexican folk art she loved. She collected about 500 small paintings called *retablos*. As a young girl, she had seen retablos at her Catholic church. They commemorate, or give thanks, for someone's miraculous recovery from illness or disaster. Imagine a thankful mother painting a retablo to honor a saint for her son's recovery from a horrible accident. It's like a thank-you note to the saint who responded to her prayers for help.

Most often, the person who requested the miracle is the one who paints the retablo. When complete, this person delivers this very personal piece of art to the church. Occasionally, an artist is hired to paint the retablo.

Retablos are small. They are most often painted on tin. They usually have three sections. At the top is a picture of the holy being that made the miracle happen. It could be a saint, the Virgin Mary, or Jesus. Puffy clouds often surround the image. In the center is a representation of the illness or disaster. It might portray the moment of the miracle. At the bottom the episode is told in words, including a note of thanks.

Many of Kahlo's paintings resemble retablos in some way. She often painted on small pieces of tin, too. Sometimes, she added words to her pictures.

Retablo

Occasionally, she made a painting as a gift in gratitude for a person's friendship. Like a retablo, it was a picture with words of appreciation.

## Sharing Her Talent: Los Fridos

Kahlo inspired young artists, too. In 1943, she and Rivera began teaching at the Academy of Painting and Sculpture. They taught high school students from poor families, who had been selected because they showed unusual artistic talent. These students were given free art supplies and tutoring by some of Mexico's finest artists and art historians. Many of the students later became famous artists in their own right.

The students called the school La Esmeralda, because that was the name of the street it was on. Kahlo and Rivera often took their students on adventures, visiting markets and neighboring cities. The purpose of these outings was to teach the young artists to draw inspiration from the everyday scenes of Mexican life. Kahlo and Rivera taught their students about Mexican art, both old and new.

Rivera's students called themselves *Los Dieguitos* ("The Little Diegos"). Perhaps because his own art education had been very structured, Rivera carefully advised his students about style and technique.

*Los Fridos*, as Kahlo's students were called, learned in a very different way. Frida insisted each student retain his or her own personality in their artwork. Preferring to allow her students to find their own style, Kahlo didn't tell them what they were doing wrong. Instead, she taught them to be self-critical.

One student, Guillermo Monroy, remembered the first day of class with Kahlo. His description appears in Hayden Herrera's book *Frida: A Biography of Frida Kahlo:*

She appeared there all of a sudden like a stupendous flowering branch because of her joyfulness, kindness, and enchantment.... She chatted with us briefly after greeting us very affectionately, and then immediately told us in a very animated way: "Well, kids, let's go to work; I will be your so-called teacher, although I am not any such thing, I only want to be your friend, I never have been a painting teacher, nor do I think I ever will be, since I am always learning.... I hope you will not be bored with me, and when I seem a bore to you, I ask you, please, not to keep quiet, all right?"

Next, Kahlo asked what they wanted to paint. This was a delightful surprise to the students who had always been *told* what to paint. After a few moments of silence, Monroy asked Kahlo to pose for them. He said Kahlo was very touched. With a slight smile, she asked for a chair and sat down to pose.

Later, Kahlo found a perfect project for her students—painting a mural. They were permitted to paint the walls of a nearby pulquería called La Rosita. A *pulquería* is a tavern that serves *pulque*, a strong drink made from the agave plant. The pulquería's customers are usually peasants or working-class people.

Rivera joined in, too. He was delighted to teach others about mural painting. The idea of painting a pulquería especially pleased him. These little buildings were truly Mexican. Many of them were filled with murals by local artists. Both Diego and Kahlo offered advice, along with paint and brushes, to the students. When the artwork was completed, they invited the whole town to a fiesta at La Rosita. (Unfortunately, this building was later torn down and the mural was destroyed.)

When Los Fridos graduated after three years, Kahlo was sad to say good-bye. But Rivera reminded her that "it is the moment in which they are going to walk alone. Even though they go their own ways, they will come and visit us always, because they are our comrades." It was true. Their students continued to visit them for many years.

## Fanny Rabel

One of Kahlo's students was a young woman named Fanny Rabel. She had many fond memories of her visits with Kahlo. "When she was ill and staying home, there were always people around," she remembered.

That was one of the things that impressed me very much—all those people, crazy people . . . artists and collectors and all kinds of friends. I looked at them with huge eyes, and Frida used to wink at me, because I was so impressed. And I remember after many years I used to tell her that I thought I was never going to be an artist, because I was too normal, and one must have to have a great personality to be a great artist. Then Frida would say, "You know why they do all those crazy things? Because they don't have any personality. They must make it up. You are going to be an artist because you have talent. You are an artist, so you don't have to do all those things."

Kahlo was right. Rabel became a professional artist—a specialist in painting children.

Diego Rivera, *Dream of a Sunday Afternoon in Alameda Park*, 1947–48

# 10 The Final Years

rida Kahlo's health began to fail soon after she started teaching at La Esmeralda in 1943. She was experiencing shooting pains in her back and right foot. She suffered from pain much of her life, but now it was much worse.

She couldn't make the long commute to the school, so Kahlo decided to hold classes at her home. Most of her students made the long trip from Mexico City to Coyoacán and the Casa Azul. Kahlo held class in her garden several times a week. But over time, the class decreased to only four or five dedicated students. These students became like a family to her.

Los Fridos enjoyed their teacher's enchanting home. They pored over her library of pre-Columbian and European art books. Kahlo also encouraged them to read classic novels and poetry. The students had plenty of models to sketch at the Casa Azul. They were surrounded by monkeys, parrots, dogs, plants, and all types of pre-Columbian art. Even though Kahlo was often in pain, she turned these sessions into little fiestas. There were always plenty of food and refreshments for her students. She liked to take them to the movies after class.

Doctors had differing ideas about how to help Kahlo. She began wearing a steel corset to support her back. One physician, Dr. Alejandro Zimbrón, thought this would make her more comfortable. Instead, Kahlo lost her appetite. She lost 13 pounds in six

months—a lot of weight on her petite frame. She felt weak, and she had fainting spells.

Next, Dr. Zimbrón decided Kahlo should receive spinal injections, but these only increased her pain. The shots gave her splitting headaches. Last, he tried to stretch her spine, by propping her in a near vertical position. He tied heavy bags of sand to her feet. She withstood this torment for three months. Throughout all of these procedures, she continued to paint for an hour every day. None of the treatments seemed to work. None improved her health or provided relief from her constant pain. Kahlo was getting desperate.

In 1946, feeling as if she had no other choice, she agreed to a drastic operation—a bone graft to help her damaged vertebrae. Her sister Cristina accompanied her to New York for the two-month ordeal. Dr. Philip Wilson removed a bone from Kahlo's pelvis. He fused it to four vertebrae, along with a six-inch metal rod. She spent the next two months recovering in the hospital. She received morphine to relieve her pain. Morphine is a powerful narcotic that can cause addiction. While Kahlo was going through this ordeal, Diego Rivera was back in Mexico City, working on his murals at the National Palace. During this time (1946) he wrote a letter to Dr. Wilson expressing his love for Kahlo, and thanking the doctor for his help. He wrote, ". . . her life is of more value to me, much more than my own." Rivera was grateful for the

Diego Rivera, *The Milliner* (Henri de Chatillon), 1944

doctor's assistance and he also wrote that he wished to "express to you [Dr. Wilson] the debt I owe you."

The surgery was a disaster. Several doctors thought the wrong vertebrae had been fused. Afterward, Kahlo was in worse condition than ever before. She also became hooked on painkillers. Soon after she left the hospital, she was encased in a steel corset covering her torso, which she wore for eight months. Her doctors told her not to paint while she recuperated. It was a wasted warning. She paid no attention to them.

The pictures Kahlo painted during this time reflect her pain and suffering. In one, painted in 1946, Kahlo expressed both her torment and hope. She titled it *Tree of Hope.* In the painting, Kahlo shows herself dressed in one of her traditional Mexican costumes. Her hair is decorated in bright red ribbons. In her hand she holds a flag that says "tree of hope, keep firm." She is sitting next to a patient who is lying on a hospital gurney. The patient is a woman with long black hair. She is lying with her back to us, wrapped in a bed sheet. The sheet fails to cover her lower back and exposes two deep, red incisions. We understand that the patient is also Kahlo, after her operation. The healthy Kahlo is keeping watch over the injured one. In this painting Kahlo is showing us her problem, while expressing her hope for recovery.

During Kahlo's medical crisis, Rivera was busy painting. He worked on several murals in Mexico City, and he painted smaller canvases whenever he could. His most famous canvases portray scenes of Mexican life, such as flower vendors carrying baskets full of blooms. He also accepted commissions for portraits. There was a strong demand for paintings by Diego Rivera.

One of the most charming portraits he painted is called *The Milliner*. Rivera posed his subject, Henri de Chatillon, in front of a mirror. We see both his front and his back. It's a fun painting because de Chatillon is poking fun at himself—wearing an amused expression, he poses in one of the lady's hats that he sells. Rivera included beautiful blooming flowers in the scene as well.

## Paying the Bills

Art lovers around the world knew of Rivera and Kahlo. Celebrities traveling through Mexico made sure they visited the Casa Azul. The guests included movie stars and famous artists. Presidents and ambassadors arrived too. In spite of her health problems, Kahlo loved holding court.

Even though their art was selling, Rivera and Kahlo had financial problems. They were always very generous with their money. They were happy to give it to needy families or artist friends who were down on their luck. As soon as Rivera was paid for a project, he bought more pre-Columbian art and gave money away. For many years, Kahlo gave her paintings as gifts. As a result, the couple didn't have much in the way of savings to help them in tough financial times. And now they were having difficulties. Kahlo's medical bills, along with the expenses of building the Anahuacalli museum, were putting a strain on their finances. In addition, they employed a cook, housekeeper, and chauffeur.

Rivera and Kahlo did whatever was needed when the bills arrived. Once, when Rivera had to pay the electric bill, he took his watercolor paintings around to sell to friends. During this time, Rivera and Kahlo began painting with sales in mind. To have more to sell, Rivera sometimes painted two watercolors a day.

Occasionally, Kahlo would send a painting to a friend who hadn't asked for one. Included would be a bill for 10,000 pesos. The painting was seldom sent back. If it was, Kahlo became very angry and ended that friendship.

In 1947, Rivera began painting what would become known as his best mural. It was on a wall at the newly built Hotel del Prado. The painting portrays the beautiful park that was located right outside the doors of the hotel. He called it *Dream of*

## Kahlo's Diary

In 1944, Kahlo received a wonderful gift. It was a book full of blank pages that was intended to be used as a diary. Its red leather cover was stamped in gold with the initials *J.K.* It had been purchased in a rare bookstore in New York, and was believed to have belonged to the famous English poet John Keats. Kahlo was delighted!

Over the next 10 years, she filled the pages with words and images. It included love notes to Rivera, whimsical ideas, and thoughts about her loneliness and pain. Occasionally, she just listed words that started with the same letter, writing them down like a poem. She wrote in many colors of ink, and drew a lot of pictures. The pages vibrate with color. She used many materials including colored pencils, crayons, inks, and paints. Sometimes, she glued a small photo on the page and embellished it with her own touches.

Some of Kahlo's images in her diary are mini portraits, still-life paintings, or landscapes. Others are pure fantasy. Kahlo liked to splash a drop of ink on the page and create an image from the shape it formed. Sometimes she plopped a dab of paint down and closed the book. This changed the shape of the dab along with creating a second spot. She added to these shapes, turning them into imaginative creatures.

# *Activity*  **Colorful Diary**

**Use Kahlo's ideas to create a journal full of fact and fantasy. Fill it with rough sketches, colorful dribbles, and playful ideas. Jot down serious thoughts or silly ramblings—whatever comes to mind, it's your creation. In her diary, Kahlo expressed both her happiness and sadness. She also loved nonsense! Add to your book over time to capture whatever mood you're in.**

## Materials

- Blank journal book, without lines and with heavy paper (an artist's sketchbook works best)
- Paint, watercolor or tempera
- Paintbrushes
- Small container of water
- Photograph of yourself
- Scissors
- Glue stick
- Color markers
- Color pencils
- Crayons
- Souvenirs such as ticket stubs or postcards

1. Start your journal with a splash! Open the book to approximately its middle. Load a paintbrush with paint and flick a dab of color onto one page. Close the book, pressing the pages together.

2. Open to the painted pages and imagine how you could use the shapes in a drawing. Perhaps they remind you of the wings of a butterfly, a two-headed sea creature, or fanciful trees in an undiscovered land. Or maybe the shapes are interesting in themselves, and you'd like to fill them with spirals, circles, and doodles. Using whatever coloring materials you'd like, add to the pages to create a picture. Now that you've broken in your book and loosened up your imagination, you're ready to start at the beginning of your colorful diary.

3. Turn to the first page of the book. This is the title page. Kahlo designed her title page using a small, unusual photograph of herself. She added a fanciful frame around the picture and drew flowers, a ribbon, and a bird. Glue a photo of yourself onto the page. Add details to create a personal design. If you like, add a few words. Kahlo wrote *Pinté de 1916* ("Painted 1916"—it's believed that this is a private joke because she would have been nine years old in 1916) in bright pink letters, at the top of her page. Perhaps you'd like to sign your name, or include a title, such as "The Great Artist Speaks."

4. The remaining pages are yours to fill up in any way you like in the days, months, and years ahead. Have fun!

Here are a few things you might try:

1. Glue a photo, postcard, ticket stub, or candy wrapper onto a page. Incorporate it into a picture, or paint on top of it. For example, attach a ticket stub from a concert. Draw the

shape of a guitar body around the ticket, adding the instrument's neck. Include symbols, such as lightning bolts, hearts, or musical notes. Add words from your favorite song, or some memories from the concert. To create a modern version of one of Kahlo's exercises you can even write a list of words that begin with the same first letter as the band's name that describe your experience at the concert.

2. Use watercolors to fill another page with color. It can be a picture of something, or simply colorful shapes. Blot the paint with a tissue so that the color is not too bold, and then let it dry. Using a bold-colored marker, write words on top of the image, perhaps words that this color brings to mind.

3. Dribble a spot of paint or ink on another page. Create an image from that shape. The picture can represent the mood you're in. For example, there are many ways to think about a spot shaped like an egg. It can be made into a teardrop on a self-portrait, a flame on a birthday candle, or the tip on the tail of a monster.

*a Sunday Afternoon in Alameda Park* (see page 118). The scene he depicted is playful, with soft, bright colors. In it, Rivera painted himself as a chubby little boy. He looks ready for mischief, complete with a frog poking out of his pocket. In the other pocket is a little snake. Rivera is holding the hand of a skeleton from the Day of the Dead. But this isn't just any calavera, it's Catrina! Dressed in her finest party dress and a big feathered hat, she also sports a feather boa. Her bony hand rests on the arm of an elegantly dressed gentleman in a bowler hat. He is Catrina's creator, Posada, a man Rivera considered one of the most significant artists of his time.

In this scene, Rivera is honoring the people who were very important to him. Behind the magical trio is Kahlo. Her right hand rests lovingly on his shoulder. Standing next to little Rivera are his two grown daughters, dressed as sophisticated ladies. Rivera was an expert at portraits, and this mural is full of them.

More than 150 people are included in *Dream of a Sunday Afternoon*, many of them famous figures in Mexico's history. One of them is Ignacio Ramirez. In the mid-1800s, he had encouraged Mexico's government to separate itself from the Catholic Church.

Nearly everyone liked the mural as they watched it come to life. But Rivera added three words to a sheet of paper the figure of Ramirez was

Diego Rivera, detail from *Dream of a Sunday Afternoon in Alameda Park*, 1947–48

holding. He wrote, "*Dios no existe!*" ("God does not exist!") This caused an uproar.

Angry Catholic students stormed the hotel. They scratched out the words and gashed the image of Rivera as a little boy. Mobs stoned Rivera's San Angel studio, breaking windows. Rivera and his friends protested in front of the hotel, and forced their way in to repair the damage. All this kept the hotel in the headlines, but it wasn't the type of publicity the manager wanted.

When Rivera refused to paint out the words, the mural was covered with a movable screen. Occasionally, if an important guest requested to see it, the hotel management took down the screen. But it would be many years before the mural would be seen by the general public. Shortly before his death, Rivera agreed to remove the words, and the mural was finally unveiled.

In August 1949, there was a retrospective exhibition of Rivera's artwork at the Palace of Fine Arts. A *retrospective* includes works from each period of an artist's career.

It was a wonderful exhibition. Five hundred pictures were gathered from museums and private collectors from around the world. Of course the murals from around the world could not be included in the exhibit; however, there were photographs and sketches of many of them. If someone wanted to see actual Rivera murals, they had only to go down the street to see buildings covered with them. In total, the exhibit included 1,000 pieces from Rivera's 50-year career. The retrospective was a huge success. Miguel Aleman Valdés, president of Mexico, called Rivera a national treasure. A year later, he received the National Art Prize.

## A Year in the Hospital

In 1950, one year after Rivera's retrospective, Kahlo spent an entire year in the hospital. She was 43 years old. The problem began when four toes on her right foot turned black. Doctors diagnosed this as gangrene, the result of poor circulation. *Gangrene* is a disease that causes the flesh on affected parts of the body to wither and die. Kahlo's leg had poor circulation. If left untreated, the gangrene could spread. In addition, the pain in her back was unbearable.

Kahlo's physician, Dr. Juan Farill, recommended another operation. Once again, a bone was grafted onto her spine in an attempt to help her damaged vertebrae. Afterward, the implanted bone caused a severe infection. Over the next several months, Kahlo had six more operations.

During the year, Rivera lived in the hospital, too. He read poetry to Kahlo, often rocking her to sleep in his arms, and entertained her with silly antics. Once when she had a terrible headache, he danced around her bed shaking a tambourine, pretending to be a bear. At night, he slept in a small room next to Kahlo's.

When she was well enough to paint, Rivera brought a handsome Huichol Indian, dressed in traditional costume, to pose for her. Descendants of the Aztecs, the Huichol Indians remain true to ancient traditions, customs, and language. They are famous for their colorful yarn "paintings." Kahlo painted while lying in bed, just as she had done when she was a teenager after her trolley accident.

As she recovered, her spirits rose. Kahlo was a great patient! The nurses adored her gaiety. Because she never complained, the doctors liked her too. Walking into her hospital room was like joining a party. It was decorated with candy skulls and doves made of wax and paper. Next to her bed were piles of books, pots of paint, and a jar of brushes.

She even decorated herself. Kahlo had to wear a plaster corset, like a cast, that extended from under her arms to her waist. She turned the cast into a piece of art, decorating it with feathers, photographs, paint, and little mirrors. The corset was often replaced, and each one was uniquely decorated. One day the doctors decided she should rest and therefore removed all her paints. Not to be stopped, Kahlo decorated her new corset using lipstick. When she spotted a bottle of iodine in her room, she used this brownish-red liquid to continue. Kahlo thought it would add a bit of pizzazz.

Friends frequently came to visit. Kahlo loved to be silly. She entertained them with her antics. She created a stage, using the metal contraption designed to raise her leg. With her feet, she put on puppet shows.

She particularly enjoyed visits from children. One nine-year-old fan came regularly. A native Indian boy named Vidal Nicolas, he would stand adoringly by her bed as she painted.

At lunchtime, Cristina would arrive with friends and a big basket of food. "There was a party on in Frida's room every day," her friend Olga Campos recalled.

"When I leave the hospital two months from now," Kahlo announced, "there are three things I want to do: paint, paint, paint." In December, the doctors declared her well enough to go home.

But once there, she found that she didn't have much energy. She was only able to paint for short periods of time. Using a cane or crutches, she could walk only a short distance. Most often, she used a wheelchair.

Despite the changes, Kahlo and Rivera tried to maintain their old traditions of hospitality. December 8, 1950, was the 10th anniversary of their second marriage. To celebrate, they held a big fiesta, inviting their friends and family. The Riveras still loved excitement and drama. Their anniversary provided the perfect opportunity for it.

## Earthquake in Mexico City

The Aztecs called their country "Land of the Shaking Earth." At 7:17 A.M. on September 19, 1985, that title was quite appropriate. A tremendous earthquake measuring 8.1 on the Richter scale rocked central Mexico. More than 8,000 people died in the quake, and approximately 500 buildings in Mexico City were severely damaged. The Hotel Prado was one of them.

Miraculously, Rivera's mural survived. However, soon after the quake, the hotel was torn down. But before the place was demolished, Rivera's huge mural was rescued. One passerby remembers seeing a large section of brightly painted wall being carried through the park by workers. The restored mural now sits nearby in a special museum—the Museo Mural Diego Rivera.

## Lola Alvarez Bravo

There were very few female Mexican artists in Kahlo's day. A photographer named Lola Alvarez Bravo was one of the best.

She was born in Jalisco, Mexico, in 1907. Orphaned at only eight years old, Lola grew up in the home of relatives. When only in her teens, she married her childhood friend and neighbor, Manuel Alvarez Bravo.

Manuel was a professional photographer, and Lola worked as his assistant. He had only one camera. Now and then, Lola used it too. It soon became apparent that she was a very talented photographer herself.

Lola was not the type to be content as someone's assistant. "When I was a girl, they taught me to serve tea, to make pastries," she said. "I didn't enjoy any of that. It was supposed that I had to know such things because I was a señorita, but to me it was denigrating [belittling]. They also wanted me to learn how to play the piano. I knew what was going to happen; at parties I would have to play so that everyone else could jump. I said no. I said that I wanted to jump as well."

Lola and her husband were part of the group of artists and thinkers involved in the Mexican Renaissance. For 37 years, Lola worked as a photographer for the Department of Aesthetic Research at the National University of Mexico. She documented ancient archeological sites and the beauty of Mexico. She also captured the spirit and beauty of the Mexican people. One of those people was Kahlo.

The two artists were very good friends, and Lola took many photos of Kahlo. For a time, Lola owned a gallery in Mexico City. Toward the end of Kahlo's life, Lola arranged a one-woman exhibit of Kahlo's work at her gallery.

For the party, they decided to reenact their wedding vows. Kahlo appeared as a bride, wearing a veil and crown. Rivera was dressed elegantly in a theatrical cape and hat. They put on a grand display as Kahlo's brother-in-law married them in a mock ceremony. When he asked if anyone knew why the two should not be married, Rivera's grown daughter, Ruth, got into the act. Tall and husky, she stole the show. Dressed as a baby and carrying a big pacifier, she shouted "Daddy! Daddy!" to everyone's delight.

### Changes in Kahlo's Style

As she grew older, Kahlo's painting changed. She didn't paint as many self-portraits, choosing still lifes instead.

And she created smaller, easier-to-paint pictures full of bright, luscious fruit. Often, she included a pet bird sitting among the fruit. Kahlo also started thinking more and more about social issues and world problems. Her still lifes included flags, political sayings, and symbols that were important to her.

Kahlo's painting technique also changed. Heavily medicated, she couldn't paint small details easily. Her style became looser, and she didn't spend as much time on each painting. Some people think she hurried to make money so that she could buy medicines or help pay bills. However, it is also true that she was on medication and didn't have the same control over her brushstrokes as she'd once had.

## An Eventful Year

Early in 1953 at age 45, Kahlo showed her paintings in a solo exhibit for the first time in her own country. Held at Lola Alvarez Bravo's gallery, it was a retrospective of her life's work. It gave a great lift to Kahlo's spirits.

Rivera personally supervised the hanging of her paintings. Although she was bedridden, Kahlo made the invitations. Still, as the preparations proceeded, Rivera was afraid Kahlo would be too ill to attend the opening. But she *did* attend—and with the kind of drama only Kahlo could dream up.

At opening night, no one was sure whether Kahlo would show up. Her doctors warned her to stay home in bed. The guests arrived, sorry to find the star of the show missing. But with her usual flair, Kahlo appeared. She arrived in an ambulance, with sirens blasting, accompanied by a motorcycle escort. Her canopied bed was set in the middle of the room, and she held court among her well-wishers. Her guests formed a long line to greet her. To *Time* magazine reporters she announced, "I am not sick. I am broken. But I am happy to be alive as long as I can paint."

Kahlo's one-woman show was a tremendous success. News about it spread across the ocean.

"We received calls from Paris, London, and from several places in the USA asking us for details about Frida's exhibition," recalled Lola Alvarez Bravo. The gallery had to extend the exhibit for a month because of popular demand. Rivera was thrilled with Kahlo's success. In his autobiography he wrote, "For me, the most thrilling event of 1953 was Frida's one-man show in Mexico City during the month of April. Anyone who attended it could not but marvel at her great talent. Even I was impressed when I saw all her work together."

That summer, she was hospitalized again. Gangrene had set in on her right foot and was spreading. Her doctors decided it was necessary to amputate her leg below the knee. They said there was no need to hurry, the gangrene would spread slowly. But they were sure that it must be done. Bravely she said, "Then amputate now." It was her 14th operation in 16 years. In her personal diary she wrote, "Feet, why do I want them if I have wings to fly?"

After the operation, Kahlo remained in the hospital for three months. She joked about her operation when friends came to see her. But when Rivera visited, he was not fooled. At the time he and Kahlo first learned that she would need this operation, he could hardly hold back his tears. He said to a friend, "She is going to die; this is going to kill her."

At the end of this three-month stay and her amputation Kahlo returned to the Casa Azul, but

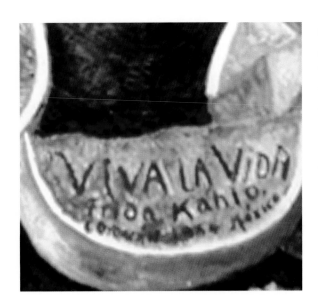

Frida Kahlo, detail from *Still Life: Viva la Vida*, c. 1951–54

she was never the same. She was seldom cheerful. Addicted to painkillers, she was quick to quarrel with those around her. Rivera did what he could to comfort her. He sat by her bedside, telling her stories and quietly singing Mexican ballads. In his autobiography he wrote, "Often, during her convalescence, her nurse would phone to me that Frida was crying and saying she wanted to die. I would immediately stop painting and rush home to comfort her. When Frida was resting peacefully again, I would return to my painting and work overtime to make up for the lost hours."

After many months of recovery, Kahlo tried to paint. She forced herself out of bed and sat at her easel. To be able to sit up for any amount of time, she tied herself to her wheelchair, to support her back. When the pain became unbearable, she returned to bed and continued painting there. Gradually, her spirits rose a bit.

Her condition may have added a sense of urgency to her commitment to social causes. She did what she could to voice her concerns. On July 2, 1954, Kahlo disobeyed her doctor's orders and went to a political demonstration. With Rivera pushing her wheelchair, she joined 10,000 others in a protest against U.S. policies in Guatemala. For four hours, Rivera and Kahlo marched with the others shouting, *"Gringos asesinos, fuera!"* ("Yankee assassins, get out!") She held a

large picture of a dove and the phrase *"Por la Paz"* ("For the Peace"). It was the last political stand she took. Kahlo went to the rally knowing she had pneumonia. It was a serious illness and even more difficult to fight in her weakened state. Her long day in the cold weather made it worse.

## Long Live Life

Although frail, she had been working on a still life of ripe red watermelons. Sliced into sections, the colors almost vibrate. The vivid green rinds contrast with the juicy red fruit. She painted a beautiful blue sky in the background.

Three days after the rally, Kahlo finished the picture. She dipped her brush in red and wrote "Frida Kahlo, Coyoacán 1954 Mexico" in one slice of melon. Then, in large letters she added *"Viva La Vida"* ("Long Live Life").

On July 13, 1954, Kahlo gave Rivera a special gift. It was a ring she had bought for their silver wedding anniversary, only 17 days away. He asked why she was giving it to him early, and she replied, "Because I sense that I'll be leaving you very soon." That night, he stayed by her bedside until she was asleep, and then went to his San Angel studio.

During the night Kahlo died. She passed away in the house where she had been born 47 years earlier.

Early the next morning a messenger brought Rivera the news. Rivera returned home to the Casa

Azul. Friends dressed Kahlo in her favorite Tehuana outfit. They draped her in jewelry and braided her hair with flowers. While this was happening, Rivera stayed in his room and refused to see anyone.

A reporter, eager for a story, tried to interview him. For once, Rivera had nothing to say. He requested, "I beg you don't ask me anything," and turned his face to the wall. Later, Rivera wrote, "July 13, 1954, was the most tragic day of my life. I had lost my beloved Frida, forever."

Kahlo's open casket was placed in the foyer of the Palace of Fine Arts—the most important cultural institution in Mexico. That day, thousands of people walked past the coffin to say good-bye to Kahlo.

The director of the Palace of Fine Arts had granted Rivera use of the premises. But knowing Rivera's ways, he stipulated that there be no political banners or speeches during the funeral. Indeed, Rivera did cause a problem. During the ceremony, the flowers on Kahlo's casket were removed and Arturo García Bustos, one of Los Fridos, draped it with a Communist flag. Kahlo would have been pleased. Even in death, she caused a stir.

## Life Without Kahlo

Diego Rivera lived three more years without his beloved Frida. One year after her death he married his art dealer, Emma Hurtado. He and his new wife accepted an invitation from the Moscow Fine Arts Academy to visit the Soviet Union. But there, Rivera checked into a hospital to be treated for cancer. Apparently, the treatment helped. He returned to Mexico in good spirits, to celebrate his 70th birthday. In commemoration, the Mexican government declared his birthday a day of national homage. He was not well, yet he continued to paint. In 1956 he completed 56 oil and watercolor paintings. He looked forward to painting more murals.

In September of 1957, Rivera suffered a stroke. As a result, he lost the use of his right arm. Still, he continued to paint.

On November 24, 1957, Rivera called for Hurtado as he rested in his room. She asked him if he wanted her to raise his adjustable bed. He replied, "On the contrary, lower it." Those were his last words. He died soon after of heart failure.

Rivera's funeral was also held at the Palace of Fine Arts. Thousands of friends, family, and Mexican citizens came to pay their respect. A huge crowd gathered to march in his funeral procession through the streets of Mexico City.

After Kahlo's funeral, she had been cremated. Later, her ashes were placed in a pre-Columbian jar. Rivera's wish was to be cremated also, and have his ashes mingled with Kahlo's. Then, the jar was to rest in a special place at Anahuacalli.

He wanted to be with Kahlo among his collection of pre-Columbian art.

His wishes were not honored. Instead, the government insisted on placing him among the great heroes of Mexico. This, they thought, was only right for their most famous artist. There was a hallowed place for men of his stature: The Rotunda of Illustrious Men. It was there Rivera was laid to rest.

Frida Kahlo, *Still Life: Viva la Vida*, c. 1951–54

# 11 The Legacy of Frida Kahlo and Diego Rivera

F rida Kahlo and Diego Rivera died nearly 50 years ago. Today their art is more popular than ever. The legacy of each of these great artists is extensive. On pages 135–136 you'll find many locations where you can enjoy their art.

## The Life Work of Frida Kahlo

It took 20 years for Kahlo's paintings to become well known in the United States. In 1978, she took Chicago by storm when the Museum of Contemporary Art featured her works in a show. It was there that many Americans saw her art for the first time, and many fell in love with it. Exhibitions in London, Germany, Japan, and France soon followed. Kahlo and her work became known throughout the world.

Since her death, Kahlo has become a symbol for women's ability to succeed. In the United States this began in the 1970s when women's issues gained prominence. Important issues for women included equality in the workplace and admission to male-dominated colleges such as Yale and Princeton. Today, Kahlo's image shows up everywhere. Maybe you've even seen her in your mail! In 2001, the U.S. Postal Service issued a stamp with an image of Kahlo's 1933 painting *Self-Portrait with Necklace*.

Many of Kahlo's collectors are women. One of her big fans is the pop singer Madonna. Because Kahlo is so popular, her paintings sell for very high prices. In 1990, her painting *Diego and I* was the first piece from Latin America to sell for more than $1 million. Its full price was $1.43 million. More recently, one of her self-portraits sold for more than $3 million.

Kahlo's life story has also inspired playwrights and screenwriters. *When Will I Dance* is a play written by Claire Braz-Valentine. The story is based on Kahlo's imaginary childhood playmate. Recovering from polio at age six, Kahlo imagined this wonderful friend as someone who could dance while she herself could barely walk. In 2003, director Julie Taymor made a major motion picture about Kahlo's life. *Frida* starred Salma Hayek and was nominated for several Academy Awards.

Fridamania has swept the United States. There are even Frida look-alike contests! When her friend Lucienne Bloch was asked what Kahlo would think about all the hype, she replied, "She would have a big laugh. Kahlo would say, 'Look at those crazy gringos!'"

Kahlo's legacy was perhaps best summed up in the words of her friend Andrés Iduarte, when he spoke at her funeral. He ended his speech with these words: "Friend, sister of the people, great daughter of Mexico—you are still alive."

Frida Kahlo, *Self-Portrait as a Tehuana* (*Diego in My Thoughts*), 1943

## What Diego Rivera Left Behind

Diego Rivera's art became increasingly popular in the years following his death. Today, his paintings hang in the world's finest museums. People from around the world visit Mexico and the United States to see his murals. Eight years before Rivera died, a writer tried to estimate how big an area his murals covered. She estimated that if each fresco were only three feet high, Diego's art would stretch two and a half miles. This amazing figure doesn't include Rivera's easel paintings or the murals he painted after 1949.

It was important to Rivera that his art be available to all people, not just collectors and museum visitors. In Mexico City, thousands of people pass his frescoes every day on their way to work and school. Almost all Rivera's murals are available for public viewing.

Rivera would be delighted by the influence his work exerted on the next generation of artists. Like him, they wielded their brushes to express concern about social issues. In the 1960s, they painted murals about the Vietnam War and the civil rights struggle. Today, murals portray all types of social concerns, from environmental issues to freedom of speech. Like Rivera, artists still paint murals celebrating ethnic pride and the dignity of working-class people.

Rivera gave the world more than his artwork. He also left several important ideas. The first is that art should be for everyone. Second, art should show the importance of common people. Third, art should be meaningful but accessible enough to be understood by every viewer. And finally, art should make people think.

Rivera's life as an artist wasn't always easy. He caused incredible controversy. But Diego's life was never boring. Everything he did, he did with gusto.

## The Casa Azul

Kahlo left the Casa Azul to the people of Mexico. Today it is called the Frida Kahlo Museum. The walls are still painted vivid blue, and huge Judas figures await visitors at the entrance. Inside, visitors will see many of Kahlo's favorite possessions. Her collection of retablos hangs on the walls, along with her own artwork. Visitors who never met Kahlo leave the house feeling they know her in some way. They see her jewelry, folk art, books, art supplies, and love notes to Rivera. In her studio, a wheelchair sits facing her easel. A decorated plaster corset sits on her four-poster bed, and a mirror is attached under the bed's canopy. Kahlo's ashes rest in a pre-Columbian vase nearby.

On the living room wall hangs *Viva la Vida*, Kahlo's last work. Her life *does* live on in her paintings and in the colorful tapestry that is the story of her life.

# Elena Climent

Elena Climent was born in Mexico City in 1955. At age 16, she decided to become a painter. Just one year later she had a major exhibit of her work.

Climent's father was an artist too. He thought that art school would spoil his daughter's natural talent. As a result, Climent is mostly self-taught. She did study for a time, however, in Mexico City, Valencia, and Barcelona, Spain.

Climent never met Kahlo, who died one year before she was born. But like Kahlo's, her paintings are filled with fantasy and emotion. She is known for her detailed still-life paintings. She paints them so realistically that they almost appear to be photographs. Her paintings are usually small and filled with many commonplace objects (much like Kahlo's often were), usually things that you might find in a modern-day Mexican home, such as a plastic toy.

Through the objects she chooses, and the way she arranges them, Climent tells a story. One example is a picture she titled *Dresser with Doll and Old Studio Photograph*. The six items displayed on a dresser top are from her parents' home. There's a house-key, some money, a small plant, and an antique doll whose cracked arm is mended. Propped next to the doll is a photograph of an artist's studio. The wall behind the table is bright yellow. It's decorated with a row of green and orange Mexican tiles. A small framed photo of a child hangs on the wall.

Looking at the painting is like snooping in a stranger's home. You wonder who lives there, and where they are now. Because they left their key and money, it seems as if they'll be back at any moment.

Climent's paintings hang in many museums, including the Phoenix Art Museum and the Milwaukee Art Museum. She lives in New York and returns to Mexico several times a year to gather inspiration for her work.

## Visit the Work of Frida Kahlo and Diego Rivera

**See Diego Rivera's murals in the following cities in the United States**

San Francisco

    City College of San Francisco

    San Francisco Art Institute

    Pacific Stock Exchange

Detroit

    The Detroit Institute of Arts

### Museums that own paintings by Diego Rivera

Arkansas Arts Center, Little Rock

Detroit Institute of Arts, Michigan

Los Angeles County Museum of Art, California

Museo Dolores Olmedo, Mexico City

Museo Nacional de Arte, Mexico City

San Francisco Museum of Modern Art, California

### Museums that own paintings by Frida Kahlo

Harry Ransom Humanities Research Center,
  University of Texas, Austin

Museum of Modern Art, New York

Madison Art Center, Wisconsin

Museo Dolores Olmedo, Mexico City

National Museum of Women in the Arts, Washington, D.C.

Phoenix Art Museum, Arizona

San Francisco Museum of Modern Art, California

### See Rivera's murals in these cities in Mexico

Mexico City

Cuernavaca

Chapingo

### Museums in Mexico that are dedicated especially to the work of Rivera and Kahlo

Diego Rivera Anahuacalli Museum, Mexico City

Museo Estudio Diego Rivera, San Angel

Museo Frida Kahlo (La Casa Azul), Coyoacán

Museo Mural Diego Rivera, Mexico City

Museum Birthplace of Diego Rivera, Guanajuato

Kahlo, 1932, Detroit

## Mexican Holidays

Learn more about popular Mexican holidays. Many people in the United States hold celebrations on these days in honor of their Mexican ancestry. See if there's a fiesta in your town!

April 30
Dia de Los Niños (Day of the Children)

Sabado de Gloria (Holy Saturday)
The day before Easter Sunday, varies yearly

May 5
Cinco de Mayo

September 16
Mexican Independence Day

November 1 and 2
Dias de los Muertos (Days of the Dead)

## Find out more about Rivera's and Kahlo's work on these Web sites

### Art Encyclopedia

http://artencyclopedia.com

Search using the keywords *Frida Kahlo* and *Diego Rivera* to view many of their paintings.

### Diego Rivera Web Museum

www.diegorivera.com

View many of Rivera's murals, including photos of his unfinished RCA building mural. This site also features a gallery of Rivera's easel paintings and video clips of the artist at work. There is also footage of Frida Kahlo.

### Diego Rivera at the DIA

www.diamondial.org/rivera/anim/index/html

See photographs of Rivera and others working on the *Detroit Industry* mural, and view details of the fresco.

### The Diego Rivera Mural Project

www.riveramural.org

Learn about the *Pan American Unity* mural at City College of San Francisco.

### Frida Kahlo and Contemporary Thoughts

www.fridakahlo.it

Current news about Kahlo, including upcoming exhibitions of her work. Also see links to news articles and a listing of dance and theater performances based on Kahlo's life and art.

### Frida Kahlo and Diego Rivera: Their Lives and Ideas Online

http://members.aol.com/sabbeth/frida.html

Additional online resources from the author of this book.

### Museo Mural Diego Rivera

www.arts-history.mx

See the many portraits Diego included in *Dream of a Sunday Afternoon in Alameda Park*, and learn more about the history of the mural.

## Other Resources

### Felice Bochman

http://bostonbuonfresco.com/

Read about prehistoric cave paintings—the first murals—and see how they inspire artist Felice Bochman. Her frescos include prehistoric cave motifs such as animals, handprints, and female figures. Using these symbols, Bochman expresses her ideas about feminine identity. Bochman credits Frida Kahlo as having influenced her artistic path.

### Elena Climent

www.mamfa.com/exh/clim1997/HH_article.htm

Read an article about artist Elena Climent and view several of her paintings.

### Hector Duarte

www.hectorduarte.com

View the work of Mexican-born artist Hector Duarte and learn how he is teaching school-children to create murals.

### Jonathan Green

www.pbs.org/now/arts/greenessay.html

In the tradition of Rivera, artist Jonathan Green's brilliantly colored paintings express cultural pride and dignity. Click on "photo essay" to view Green's art and read his stories about the traditions, celebrations, and everyday life of the Gullah, a society of African Americans who live in the Sea Islands of South Carolina and Georgia.

### Mexican American Murals

www.getty.edu/artsednet/resources/Murals/artworks.html

View seven murals: four painted by contemporary Mexican American artists and three by the artists who influenced them. Learn the history of each work and read how Rivera and the Mexican Mural Movement inspire today's artists. Great for teachers and students.

### Mexican Sugar Skulls

www.MexicanSugarSkull.com

See instructions on how to make your own Day of the Dead sugar skulls.

### Georgia O'Keeffe Museum

www.okeeffemuseum.org

Visit New Mexico's Georgia O'Keeffe Museum online to view works by this artist.

### Rufino Tamayo

www.albrightknox.org/ArtStart/Tamayo.html

View one of Rufino Tamayo's colorful paintings, learn more about his debates with Rivera and other muralists, and read suggestions for hands-on activities and discussions. Great for teachers and students.

### Throckmorton Fine Art Photo Gallery

www.throckmorton-nyc.com/index.html

View the work of several photographers who knew Kahlo and Rivera including Lola Alvarez Bravo, Nickolas Muray, Tina Modotti, and Edward Weston.

# Glossary

**Anahuacalli:** the museum Diego Rivera built to house his collection of pre-Columbian artifacts.

**Aztecs:** a group of native people that lived in central Mexico from A.D. 1370 to 1521. They were the founders of Mexico City.

**Calavera:** Spanish for "skull." Used as a symbol for the Day of the Dead.

**Capitalism:** an economic system characterized by private ownership of businesses.

**Cartoon:** a preparatory drawing used in painting a fresco.

**Chichén Itzá** (Chee-CHEN eet-SAH): an important religious and political center for the Mayan and, later, the Toltec peoples. It is located in the northern Yucatán Peninsula.

**Coatlicue** (ko-aht-LEE-kway): the stern-looking Aztec goddess of earth and war. She is traditionally depicted wearing a skirt of snakes and a necklace of human hearts and hands.

**Communism:** a system of government that eliminates private ownership of businesses.

**Corrido:** a Mexican folk song.

**Cubism:** an art movement started around 1907 by Pablo Picasso and Georges Braque that breaks a picture down into geometric shapes. Images are depicted at many different angles at once.

**Deer dance:** a ceremonial dance performed by the Yaqui people to create harmony with the deer spirits.

**Donor portrait:** a portrait of the person responsible for funding the creation of a fresco. The fresco artist includes this portrait somewhere in the mural.

**Engraving:** an impression from a surface that has been cut into with a sharp object.

**Etching:** an impression from a surface that has been altered with acid.

**Folk art:** products, such as pottery, paintings, and sculptures created by untrained artists. Objects may be functional or decorative.

**Fresco:** a picture painted directly onto wet plaster with water-based pigments.

**Gringo:** a degrading term for Americans and Britons used by people in Latin America and Spain.

**Isthmus of Tehuantepec:** an area located at the southeastern tip of Mexico.

**Judas figure:** large papier-mâché figure that often looks like a devil or skeleton. Traditionally it is wrapped in firecrackers and ignited on Sabado de Gloria.

**La Casa Azul:** Spanish for "the blue house," Frida Kahlo's family home.

**La Esmeralda:** the academy of painting and sculpture where Kahlo and Rivera taught.

**La Prepa:** the National Preparatory School, Mexico City, where Kahlo went to school.

**Landscape:** a picture of natural scenery.

**Los Dias de los Muertos:** the Days of the Dead, celebrated on November 1 and 2. (November 2 is called The Day of the Dead.) This holiday honors ancestors and friends who have died.

**Los Dieguitos:** the nickname for Rivera's students at La Esmeralda.

**Los Fridos:** the nickname for Kahlo's students at La Esmeralda.

**Los Tres Grandes** ("The Three Greats"): leaders of the Mexican Mural Movement— Diego Rivera, José Clemente Orozco, and David Alfaro Siqueiros.

**Mayans:** native people who lived in southern Mexico from about A.D. 300 to 1500.

**Mestizo:** person of mixed European and American Indian ancestry.

**Mictlan:** the Aztec spirit world.

**Milagro:** Spanish for "miracle." A tiny metal charm usually shaped like a body part (arm, heart, or leg) used to request a miraculous cure.

**Mural:** a work of art, such as a painting, applied to the surface of a wall or ceiling.

**Nahuatl:** the language of the Aztecs.

**Ofreda:** a special shrine made during the Days of the Dead to honor someone who is deceased.

**Olmecs:** known as the "rubber people," a civilization that thrived along Mexico's Gulf Coast as early as 1300 B.C. in the area that is now the states of Veracruz and Tabasco.

**Ozomatli:** the god of dance, depicted as a monkey.

**Pan de muerto:** Spanish for "bread of the dead," a special bread baked during the Days of the Dead.

**Panzón:** Spanish for "fat belly," Kahlo's nickname for Rivera.

**Pedregal:** Spanish for "stony ground," the district in Mexico City where Rivera built Anahuacalli.

**Perspective:** the technique artists use to make a flat surface look as if it has depth.

**Pigment:** a substance that is added to liquid to create colored paint or ink.

**Porfiriato:** the period when the dictator Porfirio Díaz ruled Mexico (1876–1911).

**Portrait:** a picture or sculpture of a particular person.

**Pre-Columbian:** the time in North and South America before Christopher Columbus arrived.

**Pulquería:** a tavern that serves pulque, a strong drink made from the agave plant.

**Retablo:** a small folk painting made to give thanks for a miraculous recovery from illness or disaster.

**Retrospective:** an exhibition that includes pieces from each period of an artist's career.

**Sabado de Gloria:** Holy Saturday; the day before Easter Sunday.

**Scaffold:** a temporary platform for workers to stand or sit on when working at a height above the floor.

**Self-portrait:** a picture or sculpture that an artist makes of himself or herself.

**Stetson:** a felt hat with a broad brim and high crown.

**Still life:** a picture of a group of inanimate objects arranged by the artist. It's usually set indoors and contains at least one man-made object, such as a tabletop or vase.

**Sugar skull:** a special treat made of sugar in the shape of a skull, popular during the Days of the Dead.

**Surrealism:** an art movement characterized by scenes that appear absurd or dreamlike. Originating in Europe, the movement included writers, poets, photographers, and painters.

**Tarascan:** the native language of the Tarascans, people living in an area of central western Mexico now known as Michoacán.

**Tehuana:** a woman who comes from the region in southern Mexico called Tehuantepec. Tejuanas are known for their long ruffled skirts and colorful embroidered blouses.

**Trompe l'oeil:** French for "fool the eye." Art that tricks a viewer into thinking a painted object is real.

**Works Progress Administration (WPA):** a program developed by President Franklin D. Roosevelt that gave jobs to the unemployed as a way to recover from the Great Depression. Many artists found work through the WPA.

**Xoloitzcuintli** (show-low-its-queen-tlee): a breed of dog favored by Rivera and Kahlo. Once bred by the Aztecs, these dogs have no fur.

**Xolotl:** the Aztec god of lightning. The Aztecs believed that Xolotl pushed the sun toward the ocean at sunset and guarded her during the night on her dangerous journey through the underworld. He also greeted people when they died, and accompanied them on their journey in the afterlife.

**Zapatistas:** followers of Emiliano Zapata, a leader of the Mexican Revolution.

**Zócalo:** Mexico City's central plaza where the National Palace is located.

# Bibliography

Alcantara, Isabel. *Frida Kahlo and Diego Rivera.* New York: Prestel, 1999.

Arnold, Caroline. *City of the Gods, Mexico's Ancient City of Teotihuacan.* New York: Clarion Books, 1994.

Chambers, Marlene. *Little People of the Earth.* Denver: The Denver Art Museum, 1990.

Cockcroft, James. *Diego Rivera: Hispanics of Achievement.* New York: Chelsea House Publishing, 1991.

Cory, Steve. *Daily Life in Ancient and Modern Mexico City.* Minneapolis: Runestone Press, 1999.

Cruz, Barbara C. *Frida Kahlo: Portrait of a Mexican Painter.* Springfield, NJ: Enslow Publishers, Inc., 1996.

Downs, Linda Bank. *Diego Rivera: The Detroit Industry Murals.* New York: Detroit Institute of Arts in association with W. W. Norton & Company, 1999.

Drucker, Malka. *Frida Kahlo.* Albuquerque: University of New Mexico Press, 1991.

Frost, Mary Pierce, and Susan Keegan. *The Mexican Revolution.* San Diego: Lucent Books, 1997.

Gonzales, Doreen. *Diego Rivera: His Art, His Life.* Springfield, NJ: Enslow Publishers, Inc. 1996.

Hardin, Terri. *Frida Kahlo: A Modern Master.* New York: Smithwork, 1997.

Hargrove, Jim. *Diego Rivera: Mexican Muralist.* Chicago: Childrens Press, 1990.

Helms, Cynthia Newman, ed. *Diego Rivera: A Retrospective.* New York: Detroit Institute of Arts in association with W. W. Norton & Company, 1986.

Herrera, Hayden. *Frida: A Biography of Frida Kahlo.* New York: Harper and Row Publishers, 1983.

Herrera, Hayden. *Frida Kahlo: The Paintings.* New York: HarperCollins, 1991.

www.inside-mexico.com (accessed June 7, 2004).

Kahlo, Frida. *The Diary of Frida Kahlo.* New York: Harry N. Abrams, 1995.

Lee, Anthony W. *Painting on the Left.* Berkeley: University of California Press, 1999.

Marnham, Patrick. *Dreaming with His Eyes Open.* New York: Alfred A. Knopf, 1998.

Richmond, Robin. *Frida Kahlo in Mexico.* Rohnert Park, CA: Pomegranate Artbooks, 1994.

Rivera, Diego, with Gladys March. *My Art, My Life.* New York: The Citadel Press, 1960.

Rummel, Jack. *Frida Kahlo: A Spiritual Biography.* New York: The Crossroad Publishing Company, 2000.

Stein, R. Conrad. *Mexico, Enchantment of the World.* New York: Childrens Press, 1998.

Turner, Robyn Montana. *Frida Kahlo: Portraits of Women Artists for Children.* Boston: Little, Brown & Co., 1993.

Wolfe, Bertram D. *The Fabulous Life of Diego Rivera.* New York: Stein and Day, 1963.

Zamora, Martha. *Frida Kahlo: The Brush of Anguish.* San Francisco: Chronicle Books, 1990.

# Image Credits

**Front cover**
Left: Frida Kahlo
*Self-Portrait*
1940
oil on canvas
24 ½ in. x 18 ¾ in.
Harry Ransom Humanities Research Center,
University of Texas, Austin
Reproduction authorized by the Instituto Nacional
de Bellas Artes y Literatura.
D.R. © 2004 Banco de Mexico, Museos Diego
Rivera y Frida Kahlo. Av. Cinco de Mayo No. 2,
Col. Centro, Del. Cuauhtemoc 06059, Mexico, D.F.
Middle: Frida with Diego, 1941, San Angel
Photograph by Nickolas Muray,
© Nickolas Muray Archives

Center: Frida with Diego, 1941, San Angel
Photo by Nickolas Muray
© Nickolas Muray Photo Archives

Right: Diego Rivera
*The Flower Carrier*
1935
oil and tempera on Masonite
48 in. x 47 ¾ in.
San Francisco Museum of Modern Art
Albert M. Bender Collection
Gift of Albert M. Bender in memory of
Caroline Walter
Reproduction authorized by the Instituto Nacional
de Bellas Artes y Literatura.
D.R. © 2004 Banco de Mexico, Museos Diego
Rivera y Frida Kahlo. Av. Cinco de Mayo No. 2,
Col. Centro, Del. Cuauhtemoc 06059, Mexico, D.F.

**Page i**
Frida with Diego, 1941, San Angel
See image credit for cover.

**Page viii**
Frida (Frieda) Kahlo
*Frieda and Diego Rivera*
1931
oil on canvas
39 ⅜ in. x 31 in.
San Francisco Museum of Modern Art
Albert M. Bender Collection
Gift of Albert M. Bender
Reproduction authorized by the Instituto Nacional
de Bellas Artes y Literatura.
D.R. © 2004 Banco de Mexico, Museos Diego
Rivera y Frida Kahlo. Av. Cinco de Mayo No. 2,
Col. Centro, Del. Cuauhtemoc 06059, Mexico, D.F.

**Page xi**
Rivera and Kahlo, 1938, Coyocán
Photo by Nickolas Muray
© Nickolas Muray Photo Archives

**Page xii**
Diego Rivera
*The Making of a Fresco*
*Showing the Building of a City*
1931
fresco
271 in. x 357 in.
San Francisco Art Institute
Gift of William Gerstle

**Page 2**
Diego Rivera
Detail of *The Making of a Fresco*
*Showing the Building of a City*
See image credit for page xii.

**Page 3**
Diego Rivera
Detail of *Detroit Industry*, east wall
1932–33
fresco
Gift of Edsel B. Ford
Photograph © 2001 The Detroit Institute of Arts

**Page 7**
Diego Rivera
Detail of *Detroit Industry*, north wall
See image credit for page 3.

**Page 8**
Diego Rivera
Detail of *Pan American Unity*
1940
fresco
City College of San Francisco
All rights reserved. Unauthorized public
performance, broadcasting, transmission, or
copying, mechanical or electronic, is a violation
of applicable laws.
© City College of San Francisco,
www.riveramural.com

**Page 10**
José Guadalupe Posada
*La Calavera Catrina*
c. 1910
etching

**Page 14**
Kahlo painting *The Two Fridas*, 1939
Photo by Nickolas Muray
© Nickolas Muray Photo Archives

**Page 18**
José Guadalupe Posada
*Gran calavera eléctrica* (Big trolley calavera)
1907
etching

**Page 21**
Diego Rivera painting iron ore in the North Wall
middle register
1932
Courtesy of the Rivera Archives at the Detroit
Institute of Arts
Photograph © 1986 The Detroit Institute of Arts

**Page 26**
Diego Rivera
*Self-Portrait*
1941
oil on canvas
61 x 43 cm
Northampton, Massachusetts, Smith College
Museum of Art
Gift of Mrs. Irene Rich Clifford, 1977
Reproduction authorized by the Instituto Nacional
de Bellas Artes y Literatura.
D.R. © 2004 Banco de Mexico, Museos Diego
Rivera y Frida Kahlo. Av. Cinco de Mayo No. 2,
Col. Centro, Del. Cuauhtemoc 06059, Mexico, D.F.

**Page 28**
Paul Cézanne
*Still Life with Curtain and Flowered Pitcher*
c. 1898–99
The Hermitage Museum, St. Petersburg

**Page 29**
Diego Rivera
*Zapatista Landscape*
1915
oil on canvas
56 ¾ in. x 48 ½ in.
Museo Nacional de Arte, Mexico City
Reproduction authorized by the Instituto Nacional
de Bellas Artes y Literatura.
D.R. © 2004 Banco de Mexico, Museos Diego
Rivera y Frida Kahlo. Av. Cinco de Mayo No. 2,
Col. Centro, Del. Cuauhtemoc 06059, Mexico, D.F.
Photograph © 1986 The Detroit Institute of Arts

**Page 32**
José Guadalupe Posada
*Genovevo de la O*
1910–12
etching

**Page 95**
"El Castillo" main pyramid at Toltec Chichén Itzá, Mexico
© Philip Baird/www.anthroarcheart.org

**Page 95**
Olmec Head at La Venta Park, Mexico.
© Philip Baird/www.anthroarcheart.org

**Page 96**
Dog, 200 BC/AD 300
Colima
Bequest of W. Hawkins Ferry
Photograph © 1989 The Detroit Institute of Arts

**Page 96**
Diego Rivera
Detail of *Detroit Industry*, south wall
See image credit for page 3.

**Page 99**
Design motif from ancient Mexico
stamp design of jaguar and serpent, Veracruz

**Page 99**
Male and Female Figures, 100 BC/AD 400
Nayarit
Founders Society Purchase, Henry Ford II Fund, Benson and Edith Ford Fund, Mr. and Mrs. Walter Buhl Ford II Fund, Alan, Marianne and Marc Schwartz Fund, with funds from Lois and Avern Cohn, Robert B. Jacobs, Milford Nemer, Margaret H. Demant, and Mr. and Mrs. William L. Kahn.
Photograph © 1986 The Detroit Institute of Arts

**Page 100**
Figure, 1500/900 BC
Tlatilco
Founders Society Purchase,
Benson and Edith Ford Fund
Photograph © 1986 The Detroit Institute of Arts

**Page 101**
Chacmool (two examples)
© Philip Baird/www.anthroarcheart.org

**Page 102**
Design motif from ancient Mexico
flat stamp depicting Ozomatli, God of Dance

**Page 103**
Diego Rivera
Detail of *Pan American Unity*
See image credit for page 8.

**Page 104**
Diego Rivera
Detail of *Detroit Industry*, south wall
See image credit for page 3.

**Page 105**
Coatlicue, Aztec, Tenochtitlan, c. 1487–1521,
stone, h 3.5 m
Museo Nacional de Antropologia, Mexico City
Photograph courtesy of John Mitchell

**Page 106**
Artist unknown
Glazed and painted clay pot
Capula, State of Michoacán, Mexico
Collection of Michael H. and Linda G. Margolin
Photograph by Alex Sabbeth

**Page 109**
Artist unknown (chicken shape)
Glazed and painted clay pot
Capula, State of Michoacán, Mexico
Collection of Michael H. and Linda G. Margolin
Photograph by Alex Sabbeth

**Page 111**
Sugar skulls
Photograph courtesy of Reign Trading Co.
www.MexicanSugarSkull.com

**Page 113**
Laura Sallano Linares
Papier-mâché figures (wedding couple)
State of Mexico, Mexico
Collection of Michael H. and Linda G. Margolin
Photograph by Alex Sabbeth

**Page 115**
Oscar Gonzales and Aron Castillo
Retablo
State of Guanajuato, Mexico
Courtesy of Dos Mujeres Mexican Folk Art
www.mexicanfolkart.com

**Page 118**
Diego Rivera
*Dream of a Sunday Afternoon in Alameda Park*
1947–48
fresco
4.80 x 15 m
Hotel del Prado, Mexico City
Reproduction authorized by the Instituto Nacional de Bellas Artes y Literatura.
D.R. © 2004 Banco de Mexico, Museos Diego Rivera y Frida Kahlo. Av. Cinco de Mayo No. 2, Col. Centro, Del. Cuauhtemoc 06059, Mexico, D.F.
Photograph © 1986 The Detroit Institute of Arts

**Page 120**
Diego Rivera
*The Milliner* (Henri de Chatillon)
1944
Collection of Mr. and Mrs. Marcos Micha Levy
Reproduction authorized by the Instituto Nacional de Bellas Artes y Literatura.
D.R. © 2004 Banco de Mexico, Museos Diego Rivera y Frida Kahlo. Av. Cinco de Mayo No. 2, Col. Centro, Del. Cuauhtemoc 06059, Mexico, D.F.
Photograph © 1986 The Detroit Institute of Arts

**Page 123**
Diego Rivera
Detail of *Dream of a Sunday Afternoon in Alameda Park*
See image credit for page 118.

**Page 128**
Frida Kahlo
Detail of *Still Life: Viva la Vida*
c. 1951–54
oil on Masonite
23 1/3 in x 20 in
Collection of the Frida Kahlo Museum, Mexico City
Photograph courtesy of Archivo Fotografico.
CENIDIAP-INBA. Reproduction authorized by the Instituto Nacional de Bellas Artes y Literatura.
D.R. © 2004 Banco de Mexico, Museos Diego Rivera y Frida Kahlo. Av. Cinco de Mayo No. 2, Col. Centro, Del. Cuauhtemoc 06059, Mexico, D.F.

**Page 130**
Frida Kahlo
*Still Life: Viva la Vida*
See image credit for page 128.

**Page 132**
Frida Kahlo
*Self-Portrait as a Tehuana (Diego in My Thoughts)*
1943
oil on Masonite
29 7/8 in. x 24 in.
Jacques and Natasha Gelman Collection, Mexico City
Photograph courtesy of Archivo Fotografico.
CENIDIAP-INBA. Reproduction authorized by the Instituto Nacional de Bellas Artes y Literatura.
D.R. © 2004 Banco de Mexico, Museos Diego Rivera y Frida Kahlo. Av. Cinco de Mayo No. 2, Col. Centro, Del. Cuauhtemoc 06059, Mexico, D.F.

**Page 134**
Frida Kahlo, 1932
Courtesy of the Rivera Archives at the Detroit Institute of Arts
Photograph © 1986 The Detroit Institute of Arts

**Back cover**
Top: Diego Rivera, Detail of *Pan American Unity*
See image credit on page 8.

Bottom: Frida Kahlo, *My Dress Hangs There*
See image credit on page 69.

# Map of Mexico

Tijuana

La Paz

Monterrey

GULF OF MEXICO

Guanajuato

Mexico City    Chapingo

Colima    Veracruz

Yucatán Peninsula

Cuernavaca

Isthmus of Tehuantepec

Oaxaca

# Index

# Other Books by Chicago Review Press

### American Folk Art for Kids
### with 21 Activities

By Richard Panchyk
Forewords by William Ketchum Jr.
and Mr. Imagination

"This is a unique resource that will encourage a wide range of students to reconsider what makes an object art and perhaps to reconnect with their own cultural heritages."
—*Booklist*

"Panchyk covers a broad range of categories that include pottery, quilting, and the use of 'found objects' in artwork—with numerous craft ideas related to each topic."
—*Publishers Weekly*

FOUR-COLOR INTERIOR
$16.95 (CAN $25.95) 1-55652-499-4

### Leonardo da Vinci for Kids
### His Life and Ideas, 21 Activities

Janis Herbert

Selected by the Children's Book Council and the National Council for Social Studies as a Notable Social Studies Trade Book for Young People

"Herbert incorporates biography, art techniques and history, world history, science, philosophy, and crafts into one neat package. Thoroughly illustrated and well designed, this is a fine purchase that rises above the current bounty of available books on the subject."
—*Booklist*

FOUR-COLOR INTERIOR
$16.95 (CAN $25.95) 1-55652-298-3

### Monet and the Impressionists for Kids
### Their Lives and Ideas, 21 Activities

Carol Sabbeth

A selection of Scholastic Book Clubs

Selected by the Children's Book Council and the National Council for Social Studies as a Notable Social Studies Trade Book for Young People

"An indispensable learning resource."
—*The Artist's Magazine*

Twenty-one activities explore how Impressionist artists lived and painted the vibrant life of Paris at the approach of the 20th century.

FOUR-COLOR INTERIOR
$17.95 (CAN $26.95) 1-55652-397-1

### Salvador Dalí and the Surrealists
### Their Lives and Ideas, 21 Activities

Michael Elsohn Ross
Foreword by Peter Tush, Curator of Education, Salvador Dalí Museum

"This visually stunning work enhances the body of material on the artist and his contemporaries. Eminently readable, the crisply written text is detailed and thorough."
—*School Library Journal*

FOUR-COLOR INTERIOR
$17.95 (CAN $26.95) 1-55652-479-X

**CHICAGO REVIEW PRESS**

Available at your favorite bookstore or by calling (800) 888-4741
www.chicagoreviewpress.com

Distributed by Independent Publishers Group
www.ipgbook.com